HISPANIC
HOLLYWOOD

HISPANIC HOLLYWOOD

The Latins in Motion Pictures

by George Hadley-Garcia

A Citadel Press Book

PUBLISHED BY CAROL PUBLISHING GROUP

A Citadel Press Book
Published by Carol Publishing Group

Editorial Offices
600 Madison Avenue
New York, NY 10022

Sales & Distribution Offices
120 Enterprise Avenue
Secaucus, NJ 07094

In Canada: Musson Book Company
A division of General Publishing Co. Limited
Don Mills, Ontario

Queries regarding rights and permissions
should be addressed to : Carol Publishing Group,
600 Madison Avenue, New York, NY 10022

Designed by A. Christopher Simon

Carol Publishing Group books are available at special discounts
for bulk purchases, for sales promotions, fund raising, or
educational purposes. Special editions can also be created to
specifications. For details contact: Special Sales Department,
Carol Publishing Group, 120 Enterprise Ave., Secaucus, NJ 07094

Library of Congress Cataloging-in-Publication Data

Hadley-Garcia, George.
    Hispanic Hollywood : the Latins in motion pictures / by George
  Hadley-Garcia : [foreword by Dolores Del Rio].
       p.   cm.
    "A Citadel Press book."
    Includes bibliography and index.
      ISBN 0-8065-1185-0 (paper " English language format) : $15.95. --
  ISBN 0-8065-1208-3 (paper : Spanish language format) : $17.95.
      1. Hispanic American motion picture actors and actresses.
  2. Hispanic Americans in motion pictures. 3. Latin Americans in
  motion pictures. 4. Motion pictures--United States--History.
  I. Title.
  PN1998.2.H34   1990
  791.43'028'0922--dc20   90-48016
                                                             CIP

PARA FRESIA REBECCA Y LINDA FRESIA
y en memoria de
mi abuelita Nina y mi abuelito Ruben

ACKNOWLEDGMENTS

To Ronald M. Boze, without whom this book, too, would not have been complete—heartfelt thanks, always. The same to Linda Fresia, for her help, confidence and support.

Warm thanks to three special gentlemen: Douglas Whitney, a generous and enthusiastic lover of film and glamour; the charming, knowledgeable and perfectionist Manuel Cordova, dedicated to Mexico's great actresses—Dolores Del Rio and Maria Felix—whose suggestions helped make this book as good as it could be; and to a friend indeed, Doug McClelland, a top writer, collector, nostalgist and authority on Hollywood in its heyday. Thank you, gentlemen, for your contributions and encouragement.

Special thanks are also due my editor, Allan J. Wilson, always a pro and a pleasure to work with; Sue Kutosh, an outstanding artist and individual; fellow fan and Hispanic enthusiast Eduardo Moreno; and Charlie Earle, a gem of a public relations man and a fellow fan of Hector Elizondo.

I'd also like to thank:

Dolores Del Rio; Luca Bentivoglio, Jessica H. Black, Barbara Bladen, Ira Coslow, Ken Ferguson, Jose Ferrer, Gilbert Gibson and David Corkill, Greg Gorman, Tim Grey, Rich Grzesiak, Danny Haro and Edward James Olmos, Cliff Harrington, Howard Mandelbaum, Margo, Alvin H. Marill, Ernesto Martinez, Connie Martinson, Richard Natale, Cesar Romero, David Rothel, Kevin Thomas, Lou Valentino, and Vincent Virga.

And, for their inspiration: my mother Fresia, and Sarita Montiel.

CONTENTS

Humberto Encinas

FOREWORD

by *Dolores Del Rio,* 1979

The world of actresses and actors of Hispanic origin who have worked in Hollywood is one that still remains mostly unexplored. This is true, despite the popularity and allure of all things "Hollywood!"

But the fact remains that earlier in this century, glamour, wit and comedy, as well as drama and colorful adventure, were synonymous with performers from Mexico through Central America and south to Argentina, and also including Spain, Brazil and Portugal.

The motion pictures of the silent era would have been very different without the stellar presences of my handsome cousin Ramon Novarro, of the gallant Antonio Moreno, of myself and several others, besides.

In the sound era, certain stars faded and some new ones arose. I remember my pictures of the 1930s in Hollywood with great affection. There are those who are devoted to the pictures of my *compatriota* Lupe Velez, and also to actresses like Maria Montez and Katy Jurado.

The musicals of the 1940s would have been poorer without the presence of "the Brazilian bombshell," Carmen Miranda, and the 1940s saw the rise internationally of Mexican cinema, where I had resituated myself.

The 1950s saw the rise of newer Latin actors in Hollywood, like Ricardo Montalban and Fernando Lamas.

And there have always been such durable popular favorites as Cesar Romero and Rita Moreno, people whose appearance in a film creates pleasurable recognition and anticipation.

The challenge to today's actresses and actors is to create new identities for themselves, while filling the glamorous shoes of such stars as I have mentioned.

For some years now, the *presencia hispana* in Hollywood has been in an inexplicable decline. With fresh memories of yesterday's stars — thanks to a book like this one — and with today's youthful energy, it is not unlikely that a Latin Renaissance can yet take place in Hollywood, whose worldwide influence is bigger than ever, for better or for worse.

—*Dolores Del Rio*

(1904-1983)

This Foreword was written by DDR in 1979, for my proposed book on Hispanic actors and actresses.

Photo by Dana Fineman

APPRECIATION

by *Edward James Olmos*

As the twentieth century comes to a conclusion, it has become more than apparent that the art form of this period has been motion pictures. The visual image, projected on the silvery screen, is the strongest influence on the subconscious mind which has ever been created. More people have been captivated and influenced by this craft than by any other medium in recent and not-so-recent past.

Without a doubt, more films have been created by Hollywood, and seen throughout the world, than by any other place. In fact, Hollywood (i.e. Los Angeles, California) has been responsible for the very fundamentals of filmmaking, especially so in its handling of actors and actresses, and the invention of the Hollywood movie star.

It is from this very fact that so much documentation of the social history of Hollywood has been forthcoming in the past twenty-five years. Every great movie star, or director or producer, has been profiled and exposed, for better or worse. Very few topics have been left undisturbed. This is why I found *Hispanic Hollywood* to be a welcomed, and much needed, addition to the literature which already exists about the Hollywood motion picture scene. It is, in a phrase, about time.

The Hispanic community has always played an important part in the social structure of Los Angeles. It's no wonder we find Hispanics playing a major role in the creation of the Hollywood motion picture industry, particularly when silence was golden. When films were silent, there was no racial prejudice. Many of the great starring and supporting actors and actresses were of Hispanic origins.

But as this wonderful book so clearly and accurately documents, as the Hollywood motion pictures learned to talk, they also learned to stereotype, and thus gave birth to a distinctly condescending attitude toward Hispanic actors and actresses. The path the Hollywood industry took in its treatment and its portrait of Latinos is valiantly depicted here by the author.

As time has gone by, only an isolated few have been able to explore the entertainment craft on all levels of production, as a whole it has gotten no better for the Hispanics in Hollywood. Things are far from ideal, but as a group we can no longer be dismissed or ignored by the Hollywood film community or the entertainment industry. The road, thus far traveled, needed to be documented and explored. Fortunately, it has been accomplished here in *Hispanic Hollywood* and for this I am very grateful.

—Edward James Olmos

Maria Montez
©Sue Kutosh 1990

INTRODUCTION

"At first, for a long time, screen Hispanics were bandits or lovers. Then we were ignored. Today we are underrepresented, and often misrepresented, but due to our increasing numbers, we are ignored less and less . . ."
                    —*Ricardo Montalban* on
                    Univision TV network, 1988

Once upon a time in Hollywood, there were major Hispanic stars. It was a time when foreign accents and backgrounds didn't really hamper a career—look at Garbo, Boyer, Miranda, Del Rio—and when women held their own at the box office. It was also a time when movies were about human beings, as opposed to robocops, indestructible slashers and aliens from outer space. *Adult* human beings, at that, not just kids, teens and college students.

The lowest common denominator wasn't yet a sacrosanct commercial goal, and films could be made about other cultures, other eras, other people.

"Old movies had more glamour and variety," feels Raquel Welch (née Raquel Tejada). "There was more exoticism." In Welch's opinion, "The most glamorous figure in films was Rita Hayworth as

GILDA. Who was ever more appealing, and without once taking her clothes off?"

Interestingly, Welch, a love goddess of the '60s and '70s, describes a love goddess of the '40s and '50s with whom she had more in common than uncommon sex appeal. Hayworth, born Cansino, was a Hispanic actress who early on changed her surname and then became a star. Welch, a few decades later, knew to change her surname before becoming an actress.

The difference between the two women was that Hayworth never really got to explore her heritage, on-screen or off- (despite some superficial Latina or Spanish roles). Welch in the 1960s was quoted as saying about a friend, "Why, he's as Irish as you or me" (she took her surname from her first husband). But by the 1980s, she was appearing on the Phil Donahue show, discussing Central American politics—opposing Reagan's interventionism—and her Bolivian father.

One difference between today's films and those of Hollywood's Golden Age is that the 1946 GILDA was set entirely in Argentina and Uruguay, mostly in Buenos Aires. It was of course a mainstream picture. Had GILDA been made in the '70s, '80s or today, you can bet it wouldn't be set south of the border. Former Columbia film executive Leon Y. Velez notes, "The men who run Hollywood don't believe American audiences want to learn about foreign places or experiences.

"Nor do they believe audiences are interested in stories about foreigners within the United States—about immigrants and their struggles or happiness."

GILDA was typical for its day in that it cast a Hispanic star in a non-Hispanic role. And though set in South America, almost none of the supporting actors portraying local characters were Hispanic. They were Anglo, Italian, German, Ukrainian, even Maltese and Rumanian!

It was routine for performers with Hispanic surnames to find themselves—unless they were stars—restricted to films with foreign, usually Latin, settings. And often to play no more than part of the setting. For instance, Mexican dancer-actress Margo (who'd trained with Margarita Cansino's father) made very few films—14 in 30-odd years. Even though she'd played a pivotal role in the 1937 LOST HORIZON, Margo recalled:

Ana Alicia

Trini Alvarado

14

Cantinflas

Ruben Blades

"They didn't know what to do with us. With *me*, in particular. Me and my one name! Most of the time, we were viewed by the producers as 'local color.'"

A talented performer, Margo didn't fit the mold of "Spanish" seductress. Whether set in Mexico or South America, a love story had a seductress unthinkingly called "Spanish," due to her whiteness; if not pale-skinned, an actress didn't get to play a seductress. Also, Margo had too much dignity to play that other *Hispana* stereotype, the clown. No wonder Hollywood didn't know how to categorize and therefore employ her.

The problem is an ongoing one. Says actor Jorge Velazquez, "If they can pigeonhole you, you can be employed. But is it worth it? The thing is, you'll play the same stereotype over and over and over."

Because foreign accents and exoticism were more acceptable in actresses, early Hollywood had more female Hispanic stars than male ones. And though typically cast as "hot-blooded" types—therefore more limited than their European sisters—Latinas did play the upper end of the social scale in those days.

Vikki Carr

For instance, Maria Montez and Carmen Miranda, who perfectly incarnated the temptress and the clown, respectively. In those days, with more movies being made, and more of them set in foreign locales, a well-played stereotype could translate into a stellar career and lasting fame—as Montez and Miranda illustrate, their popularity continuing today via television, cable, videocassette and arthouse revivals.

Current Hispanic actors, and more so actresses, find roles fewer and farther between. Nor are Latin characters as casually accepted as of yore. According to Leon Y. Velez, "Now, a Hispanic character has to be *explained*. A character being Hispanic isn't just taken for granted, it's often an *issue*. Usually a social and economic issue."

Barbara Carrera

Hector Elizondo

Dolores Del Rio

Emilio Estevez

Maria Felix

He adds, "Audiences still don't differentiate between the nationalities and sub-cultures within the Hispanic and Spanish-speaking world."

In that regard, it was worse in the past, when there wasn't even a distinction between Hispanic and Spanish. If one spoke Spanish—or one's forebears did!—one was adjudged "Spanish," which corresponds to calling anyone who speaks English "English," whether British, American, Australian or South African. Spanish actors sometimes objected to being lumped together with Latin Americans, while Carmen Miranda, a proud Brazilian, frequently complained, "Everybody thinks I am Spanish. Or Mexican. Or Cuban or Peruvian or . . ." This, despite her insistence on playing Brazilian characters in virtually every film.

Today, the greater numbers and visibility of Hispanics and Hispanic-Americans in the U.S. have made people somewhat more aware of the vastness and textures of the Hispanic world. As have nightly newcasts about trouble-plagued Central America and drug-ridden Colombia, not to mention Hispanic ghettos in American cities. Increasingly, TV series include Latino characters and issues, even though still under-representing what is now the nation's largest and fastest-growing minority.

Yet the small screen is years ahead of the big screen, which does however include and integrate blacks in a way most Hispanic performers aspire to. Black characters and actors have gone from being either invisible or invariably stereotyped (as menials, at the bottom of the social scale) to positions of prominence and frequency. Not so Spanish-speaking actors and characters. Or, rather, Spanish-speaking actors. For, one has to distinguish—because Hollywood did—between prominent and prized Hispanic actors and the low-down majority of Hispanic characters (often played by non-Hispanic actors).

Golden Age director George Cukor explained, "Ramon Novarro was once a guaranteed moneymaker for MGM. He said that Hollywood depicted Latin characters as scoundrels or sensualists. The men were all scoundrels, the women all sensual—which in those days meant 'sinful.' So naturally, a star like Ramon was instead cast as a hero. A hero who was probably any nationality *except* Latin American."

Post-Novarro and -Antonio Moreno (another silent star) talkies witnessed the very active careers of Gilbert Roland and Cesar Romero, then the rise of Anthony Quinn, Ricardo Montalban and

Fernando Lamas. The women were further represented by Dolores Del Rio, Lupe Velez, Katy Jurado and Rita Moreno. Hispanic stars' roles were sometimes one-dimensional, occasionally demeaning, but they were varied, they were frequent, and as often as not, they were affluent.

Nowadays the *barrio* is such an ingrained part of popular thinking about Hispanic culture that it is difficult for most Hispanic performers to escape it. Actress Dyana Ortelli recently told Hollywood's Hispanic organization NOSOTROS, "I've had it with stereotypes, with scripts about the poor, struggling Chicano people of the barrio.

Andy Garcia

Rita Hayworth

Julio Iglesias

18

Raul Julia

Carmen Miranda

Ricardo Montalban

Maria Montez

19

Sarita Montiel

Rita Moreno   Edward James Olmos

Elizabeth Peña

Ramon Novarro

Anthony Quinn

Duncan Renaldo

"Some say I've been lucky. I have worked. I played cocaine dealers, a poor barrio mother, a decent but poor Chicano girlfriend of a poor, bad and uneducated Chicano boxer, a Tijuana hooker, a poor Mexican village girl, a homeless Tijuana beggar woman, and a suffering barrio mother of a juvenile gang member . . . All poor, all uneducated, and most of them named Maria."

Other Hispanic actors have made the point that though there are now more films like LA BAMBA, STAND AND DELIVER and THE MILAGRO BEANFIELD WAR, the roles tend to remain the same. Bigger, perhaps, but the same—i.e., impoverished, semi-literate farm workers in LA BAMBA, impoverished, socially disadvantaged barrio kids in STAND AND DELIVER, and yet more dirt-poor farmers in MILAGRO BEANFIELD WAR.

Hollywood has failed to look for the varieties of *Hispanidad*, at real-life Hispanics who are affluent, educated, middle- or upper-class, who are creative or light-skinned, who are gay or don't speak Spanish, who have 1.5 (not 5.1) children or are blond or Jewish or don't have "Spanish-sounding" surnames. These roles and stories remain to be written, and most likely will have to be written by Hispanics.

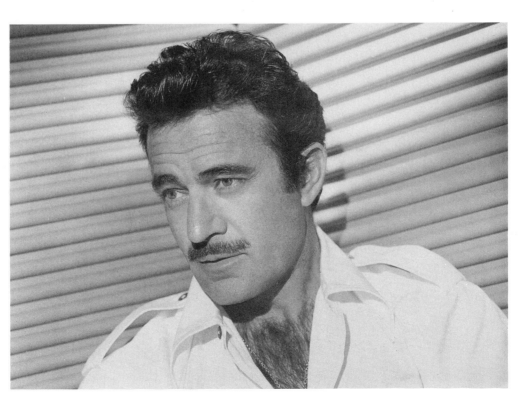
Gilbert Roland

Cesar Romero

Linda Ronstadt

Though today there are no major Hispanic (or Brazilian) stars, there is a large crop of talented, diverse and rising young Hispanic actors. Again, some may play mostly Hispanic roles—usually stereotypes, and especially if the actors are darker-skinned—but their looks, personalities and drive promise to make stars in the 1990s of, among others, Andy Garcia, Jimmy Smits, Daphne Zuñiga, Steven Bauer, Ruben Blades, Ana Alicia, Eddie Velez, Elizabeth Peña and Robby Rosa.

"We have numbers on our side," says veteran stage and film star Raul Julia. "Already we are an economic power, and a growing one. Someday, everyone will realize it." However, it's up to Hispanic audiences and the burgeoning numbers of Hispanic performers and creative artists to channel that clout into true, varied and enlightening stories about the Hispanic *experiences* . . .

Robby Rosa

Martin Sheen

Jimmy Smits

Daphne Zuñiga

Raquel Welch

Antonio Moreno and Greta Garbo in THE TEMPTRESS (1926)

1. SILENTS:
Golden Age or Tarnished?

"They say silence is golden, and for actors of Hispanic origin, silent movies were wonderful. We were not limited by our voices or accents, so Hollywood welcomed us with open arms. It has never been the same, since."
    —Ramon Novarro in *Picture Screen*, 1960

Throughout the 1920s, Latin "types" were the rage of Hollywood, led by Italian Rudolph Valentino but including Mexican Ramon Novarro and Gilbert Roland, Spanish-born Antonio Moreno, and Ricardo Cortez, a Jewish Austrian who'd changed his name from Jacob Krantz—such was the Latin Lover's commercial allure.

Nor were the Roaring '20s male-fixated, for they saw the debuts and rise of Dolores Del Rio and Lupe Velez, the most successful Mexican actresses ever to work in Hollywood.

Foreigners in general were in great demand during a decade which saw the maturation of moving pictures and an unprecedented influx of immigrants. Never again would foreign names and faces—if not voices—so dominate the silver screen. The imports included everyone from Pola Negri and Vilma Banky to Greta Garbo, who in her first two films—both based on stories by Blasco Ibañez—was paired with Moreno and Cortez.

Foreign names created audience interest, and although Luis Antonio Damaso de Alonso changed his to Gilbert Roland, Winnifred Hudnut became Natacha Rambova, and Muriel Harding evolved into Olga Petrova. Foreign was definitely *in*, and hadn't gone totally *out* by the early '40s, when Peggy Middleton opted for Latin box office appeal as Yvonne de Carlo.

(On the other hand, Charlie Chaplin successfully sued a Mexican comedian named Charles Amador who in the '20s became Charles Aplin. Yet he was unable to obtain legal remedy when a German comic resurfaced as Charlie Kaplin.)

Antonio Moreno (né Antonio Garrido Mon-

teagudo y Moreno) was the first Spanish-speaking star, a pre-Valentino Latin Lover whose screen debut was in 1912. One year later, he appeared in one of the first full-length silents, JUDITH OF BETHULIA. In the late teens, he starred in serials like THE PERILS OF THUNDER MOUNTAIN and THE INVISIBLE HAND. Moreno's stardom was boosted by a relationship with top director William Desmond Taylor, just as Moreno later helped a struggling Ramon Novarro, whom he once hid in his car in order to get him inside the studio.

Moreno's more popular films included THE TRAIL OF THE LONESOME PINE, THE SPANISH DANCER (both 1923), TIGER LOVE (1924) and HER HUSBAND'S SECRET (1925). Decades later, Moreno told an interviewer, "I was promoted as what you now call a sex symbol, though I did nothing to encourage this perception on the part of the press or the public. But Americans wanted to believe that people of Latin origins are more naturally 'spicy.'"

His final movie was John Ford's 1956 THE SEARCHERS, capping a career in which for 15 years he'd played silent leads before moving down the credits to roles as priests, judges and aristocrats. Moreno (1886-1967) told *Motion Picture* magazine

Antonio Moreno in MARE NOSTRUM (1927) with Mademoiselle Kithnou (above), May McAvoy and Fernand Mailly

in 1924, "I am not Latin American, but in the North American mind, it's all the same. North Americans don't even distinguish between a Spanish and Italian name, if it ends in *o* or *a*."

Thus, Moreno and others traveled from pictures set in sunny Spain or romantic Italy to ones in the Old West or down Mexico way and points further south. Such performers didn't have a distinct national or ethnic identity as far as Hollywood was concerned. They were simply lumped together as "foreigners." But not *too* foreign—after all, they were silent.

Ramon Samaniegos (first name José) made his screen debut in 1916. In 1921, in A SMALL TOWN IDOL, he became Ramon Novarro (1899-1968). He was seen in the first Valentino hit, THE FOUR HORSEMEN OF THE APOCALYPSE (1921) and the following year in THE PRISONER OF ZENDA. Metro, not yet amalgamated into MGM, acquired him as the studio's answer to Paramount's Valentino; after the Italian struck gold as THE SHEIK, the Mexican was starred as THE ARAB. The dashing Novarro became Hollywood's number two male sex symbol—despite their competition on-screen, off-screen Valentino and Novarro were close friends.

"Ravishing Ramon" went from triumph to triumph during the '20s, in pictures like SCARAMOUCHE (1923), BEN-HUR (1926, the most expensive silent ever made), THE STUDENT PRINCE (1927) and THE PAGAN (1929), in which he played a Polynesian. Pre-talkies, the Durango native played almost everything but Hispanic: French, German, Italian, Judean . . .

Such was also the case with his cousin Dolores Del Rio (née Lolita Dolores Martinez Asunsolo y Lopez Negrete), whom Novarro didn't meet until they were both stars in Hollywood. In 1978, Del Rio informed the author, "Skin tone was very important then, and Spanish-speaking actors in Hollywood fell into two categories. If light-skinned, they could play any nationality, including American. Dark-skinned actors were fated to play servants or appear as villains." Not even servants very often, as those were frequently enacted by blacks or white actors in blackface.

Del Rio (1904-1983) and her family narrowly escaped Pancho Villa's rebels in Durango in 1909. Reportedly the daughter of a bank president, she claimed to have been presented at the Spanish royal

Dark-complectioned Warner Baxter often played Hispanics or Indians, as in RAMONA with Dolores Del Rio (1928)

José Crespo with Dolores Del Rio in REVENGE (1928)

29

court at 14. At 21, she was discovered by a Hollywood director searching for "a female Valentino." She debuted in the 1925 film JOANNA and in 1927 starred in THE LOVES OF CARMEN. By the time sound came in, she had established herself in varied, popular and often aristocratic roles (this contrasted with the equally beauteous Lupe Velez, whose "Mexican Spitfire" image limited her roles and her prestige . . .).

Novarro and Del Rio personified another fact about certain Hispanic performers of that time—they hadn't worked their way up, but were of the aristocracy and had turned to films as a diversion. Hollywood's fascination with such porcelain-featured stars stemmed partly from their classy backgrounds, which they no doubt embellished (even Carmen Miranda would later claim that her barber father had been a fruit-export tycoon!).

By comparison, Gilbert Roland (born 1905) always acknowledged his father as a proud though

Douglas Fairbanks Sr. and Lupe Velez in THE GAUCHO (1928)

Douglas Fairbanks Sr. as DON Q., SON OF ZORRO (1925)

Fairbanks played Zorro as a swashbuckler, but in 1981, in ZORRO, THE GAY BLADE, George Hamilton played him as a cartoon

humble bullfighter. He would have been one too, had not Pancho Villa attacked his hometown of Juarez. This prompted the family's move to Texas, and in 1923 Roland bowed on screen, initiating possibly the longest film career of any Hispanic actor in Hollywood. His combination of looks and machismo enabled him to assume roles as both romantic icon—opposite superstar Norma Talmadge in 1927's CAMILLE—and tough guy—culminating in his 1940s turns as the Cisco Kid.

But somehow, that idol-making role always eluded Roland, and he didn't approach the stardom of Novarro or Moreno. Some believed his big career mistake was having changed his name!

Del Rio recalled, "The '20s were the most excit-

ing time, when several of us began in Hollywood. In a sense, they were our heyday. It was fun and new, and the doors were open to us. But I never imagined I would still be working, so long after!"

The prominence of the aforementioned Spanish-speaking actors would influence the self-image of Hispanics for a long time to come. With their individuality, appeal and innate dignity (excepting perhaps the flamboyant "hot tamale" Lupe Velez), these stars were on-going role models for young Hispanics and good ambassadors for the Hispanic heritage. That is, *when* they were perceived by the public as Hispanic, and not "European."

In the 1960s, Rita Hayworth was quoted in the Spanish magazine *Cinemundo*, "I loved the movies of Dolores Del Rio, and also Lupe Velez . . . I didn't fantasize that I would ever become a star like them, but I also didn't think I couldn't make it with the name I was born with. I don't know why that changed . . . I think it had to do with the Great Depression.

Greta Garbo and Ricardo Cortez in THE TORRENT (1926)

31

Ramon Novarro and May McAvoy in BEN-HUR (1926)

"During bad times, everything gets tougher, including people."

Sadly, the personas of Moreno, Novarro, Del Rio, Roland and Velez were atypical of the vast majority of Hispanic screen depictions. Moreno et al. routinely portrayed "good guys," but most characters from south of the border were written as "bad guys." Why? Historical competition between the U.S. and Mexico was one explanation. Yet even after the former's annexation of Texas, California, etc., the American media were quick to mirror bigotry, and were easily inflamed by bandit raids into U.S. territory, led by the likes of Pancho Villa.

In his book *The Bad Guys*, William K. Everson noted, "The Mexican villain was not only convenient, but logical—just as the German or Japanese villain became a matter of course in wartime." He added, "Even when a Western didn't use a Mexican villain, it often took pains to point out that the

Ramon Novarro as BEN-HUR and Francis X. Bushman as Messala

Ramon Novarro in scenes from BEN-HUR, the most expensive silent movie ever

Ramon Navarro as BEN-HUR with Gladys MacDowall (left) and May McAvoy

Lupe Velez in WOLF SONG (1929)

Texan or Arizonan badman was as bad as a Mexican."

Another reason for Hollywood's overwhelmingly negative depictions of Hispanics was blatant racism. The 1910s and '20s were a time when racial stereotypes were at their worst, when a hit film like D.W. Griffith's BIRTH OF A NATION could posit the Ku Klux Klan as heroes, and when screen star Anna May Wong was never allowed to kiss her Caucasian leading men.

Western star William S. Hart declared in the '20s, "Most Americans distrust our southern neighbors, on account of they're darker and shorter. They are viewed as a race apart, as well as a past foe." Hart to some degree softened the image of Native Americans in his popular Westerns (unlike "Indian" villains in the films of Tom Mix, John Wayne and others).

Ironically, one of Hart's 1916 vehicles, HELL'S HINGES, introduced the first all-American villain in a Western featuring Hispanic characters. But if this was equal opportunity villainy, it was a backhanded compliment, for a movie title explained that the Yankee badman "combined the deadly cunning of the rattlesnake with the oily craftiness of the Mexican."

Westerns were easily the worst offenders in their use of Mexican villains, for films set in urban America never included Hispanics, and non-Western stories set in Latin America were virtually non-existent. Romanticized tales of Early California tended to bypass mestizos and dwell on Anglo settlers or the ruling European Spaniards. Whenever Hollywood cast Hispanic actors as Native Americans, Spaniards or "half-breeds"—i.e., Dolores Del Rio in the 1928 classic RAMONA—they were inevitably light-skinned. (The 1936 remake starred Loretta Young.)

Del Rio later revealed, "I tried to interest my producers in stories about Mexico. I wanted to play a Mexican. But they preferred me to play a Frenchwoman or Polynesian . . . There was a strong resistance to dwelling on a performer's national heritage."

And for a time, there was even resistance to things and persons Spanish, for 1918 saw the sudden outbreak of the *Spanish* influenza, an unexplained disease which killed more people than died in the Great War, as it was called. The disease killed young, healthy individuals as well as the aged, and

Lupe Velez, the "Mexican Spitfire"

caused millions to stay away from cinemas; it was believed that one could contract the disease in crowded places.

Another cinematic double standard was that a Latina character could have a lasting affair with an Anglo male character, but not with one of her own kind. The so-called "greaser" frequently lost his female love interest to the Anglo leading man-cum-hero before fadeout. Invariably, the woman wooed and won was fair-skinned—ergo desirable in Hollywood terms—and the losing male was dark-skinned.

The greaser-loses-his-woman theme was highlighted in a series of films with titles like THE MEXICAN'S REVENGE (1909), HIS MEXICAN BRIDE (1909), THE MEXICAN'S JEALOUSY (1910) and CARMENITA THE FAITHFUL (1911). Occasionally a *malinchista* (one who esteems Yankee ways above her own) even sold out her family for the Anglo hero, as in HIS MEXICAN SWEETHEART and CHIQUITA THE DANCER, both 1912.

Bebe (née Virginia) Daniels (1901-1971)

Bebe Daniels and Gilbert Roland in THE CAMPUS FLIRT (1926)

of 1988's MOON OVER PARADOR, another picture in which the very available Latina is won by a visiting Gringo.

Occasionally the greaser was less than an out-and-out villain, and could "redeem" himself by siding with his northern neighbors. In TONY THE GREASER (1911), for instance, the title character saves a landowner's daughter from lecherous Mexican bandits. Although killed, Tony is permitted to kiss the young white woman's handkerchief as he dies! A movie ad explained Tony thus: "From force of habit, some might call him a 'Greaser;' true, he is a Mexicano, but a man of noble instincts and chivalrous nature." Therefore an exception to most greasers.

Even when less than vile, the greaser image subjected Hispanics to ridicule. Almost invariably he was an idiotic incompetent, on top of being a ruthless villain whose vices outstripped those of paler movie villains. The tendency was to depict Hispanics of both genders as funny—to be laughed at—and the men as cruel and shiftless, with the women sexy and shiftless. The depressing greaser phenomenon was abetted by such hits as THE GREASER'S GAUNTLET (1908), THE GIRL AND THE GREASER

Bebe Daniels, silent star of Spanish origin

The Latin-lover-as-loser theme was eventually pushed further south to include Panama in THE NE'ER-DO-WELL (1923), Argentina in ARGENTINE LOVE (1924) and the fictitious Paragonia in THE AMERICANO (1916)—the latter name reminiscent

36

(1913), THE GREASER'S REVENGE (1914), BRONCO BILLY AND THE GREASER (1914) and THE GREASER (1915). Said Ramon Novarro, "The greaser was too popular to be successfully opposed by anyone in Hollywood. I, among several others, made strenuous objections to my studio and others. But we could not argue with financial success."

As an unwitting representative of Latin Americans, the greaser was particularly damaging, for he was routinely shown as a sadist. For example, in THE COWBOY'S BABY (1910), he throws the hero's child into a river, while in A WESTERN CHILD'S HEROISM (1912), the greaser attacks the Americans who'd saved his life. The connection of violence and Hispanics in the public's mind was further reinforced by Hollywood's exploitation of the Mexican Revolution, which began in 1910.

(Allen Woll pointed out in his essay "The Latin Image in American Film" that "The term 'greaser' swiftly supplanted 'Mexican' or 'Latin' as a synonym for the violent Hispanic.")

"Ravishing Ramon" Novarro, Hollywood's No. 2 Latin Lover, after Valentino

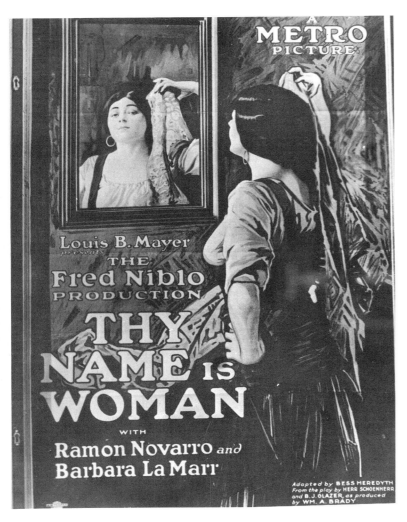

So pervasive was the impact of silent screen propaganda that moviegoing Americans often expressed more prejudice toward Hispanics than Americans less exposed to the cinema. This, according to a survey conducted for a Puebla, Mexico-based outfit called Corrientes del Cine (Cinema Currents). The U.S. trade journal *Moving Picture World* reported that audiences attending a 1911 film, ACROSS THE MEXICAN LINE, "applauded almost every move made by the good Americans, while the actions of Castro, the bandido, met with loud hisses."

(Nowadays a villain named Castro might elicit hisses for another reason. In fact, after Fidel Castro's takeover of Cuba, "I Love Lucy's" Ricky Ricardo had to change nationality. In the series' last two episodes, he was Mexican, for CBS wouldn't countenance a sitcom hero from a Communist-ruled nation!)

In his essay "The Cinematic Degradation of the Mexican, 1894-1947," Arthur G. Pettit claimed that throughout that era the Mexican was "someone to be killed or mocked, seduced or redeemed by Saxon protagonists."

Of all the minority groups libeled in early silents, Mexicans were among the first to complain, due to the stereotypes' viciousness. But the complaints fell on the deaf ears of the Republican Taft administration. Woodrow Wilson, who entered office during

Novarro's silent love stories earned him fans of all ages and nationalities

World War I, was more sympathetic. On behalf of Mexican-Americans and the Mexican government, he "asked the movie-men to please be a little kinder to the Mexicans."

A few producers heeded Wilson, with the result that their Westerns began exclusively to feature Native American villains, instead. Like the Mexican with his colorful costume and sombrero, the Native American's garb made him stand out from the American hero without even having to wear black.

During WWI, the greaser was semi-retired while Hollywood went to work on Germanic villains—the "dirty Hun" who threatened Anglo-American hegemony. Once the war ended, the celluloid ceasefire against Mexicans was called off, and the greaser was back, as in 1918's GUNS AND GREASERS. By 1919, the Mexican government had had enough, and formally complained about Hollywood's delib-

Hollywood newcomer Dolores Del Rio relaxes on the lot

erate focus on the "worst conditions they could find." The official letter of complaint also warned that U.S. production companies might be restricted from filming in Mexico.

The righteous epistle did not deter Hollywood in its quest for quick profits, and in 1922, the Mexican government went ahead and banned movies featuring derogatory depictions of its citizens: "The usual portrayal of the Mexican in moving pictures is a bandit or a sneak. Ill will toward Mexico has been inflamed by these pictures to such an extent that the government finds it necessary to make such a protest."

When Mexico realized that banning a single film here or a film there did not faze the major studios, it proposed a ban on *all* movies produced by an offending studio. Hollywood took pause at the thought of losing the entire Mexican market, and the government of Panama followed Mexico's example with similar restrictive legislation.

But the main result was that the greaser lost his nationality, if not his recognizability as an Hispanic. He was no longer called a "greaser." Hollywood complied with the letter of the foreign laws, but few were fooled. For instance: the 1927 THE DOVE (co-starring Gilbert Roland) featured Noah Beery as Don José Maria y Sandoval, who deemed himself

Mexican Dolores Del Rio was one of Hollywood's top ten moneymakers during the 1920s

Newcomer Dolores Del Rio

Through the '20s, the number of Hispanic characters dropped, especially after 1926, when the death of Valentino curbed even the demand for Latin Lovers. Greasers and other stereotypes weren't replaced by Hispanic good guys. Hispanics were more or less forgotten until the advent of sound, when their accents would again make them "funny" and "strange" to mainstream audiences.

The anomaly was that when other nations protested negative portrayals of their people, Hollywood could respond with, "Well, look at REMBRANDT or LOUIS PASTEUR," and the Dutchman or Frenchman was mollified. There were no such offsetting positive portraits of famous Hispanics. The first biofilm of a Hispanic national hero wouldn't appear until 1939, with (Benito) JUAREZ predictably impersonated by a non-Hispanic actor.

The Mexican Revolution was an excellent source of high drama and coincided with the first decade of full-length motion pictures. But although Hollywood didn't overlook this historic event occurring not far from its doorstep, it squandered its dramatic potential. Of 15 American films with Mexican settings released between 1913 and 1916, five didn't

"the bes' dam' *caballero* in Costa Roja." The title cards indicated that the fictional Costa Roja was located in the Mediterranean.

The New York Times' Mordaunt Hall wrote, "José is perhaps a screen character to which (sic) the Mexican government might have objected, for he is greedy, sensuous, boastful, cold-blooded, irritable and quite a wine-bibber, but he does dress well. He hates to have his luncheon spoiled by a noisy victim of his shooting squad." When THE DOVE was remade in 1932 as the talkie GIRL OF THE RIO with Dolores Del Rio, Hollywood moved the setting from the Mediterranean to a Mexican bordertown, inflaming the Mexican and several other Latin governments.

As greasers declined in frequency in America, they picked up popularity in Germany. German-made American-style Westerns flooded European markets with Mexicans as hackneyed villains with swarthy complexions, droopy mustaches, guns in their nervous hands, and "Caramba!" as the unvarying first word in every otherwise German sentence.

Dolores Del Rio vamps Don Alvarado in THE LOVES OF CARMEN (1927)

Dolores Del Rio as a gypsy bear-tamer in REVENGE (1928)

Dolores Del Rio in a Russian mode in THE RED DANCE (1928)

Dolores Del Rio as RAMONA (1928)

include American characters but only alluded to the Revolution, five focused on American characters and ignored the Revolution, and five simple-mindedly presented the U.S. army avenging Mexican bandit-rebels.

These 15 were far outnumbered by movies not set in Mexico but deploying pernicious Mexican characters.

One of the better Revolution pictures was THE MEXICAN JOAN OF ARC (1911), initially about a father and son arrested as *insurrectos* and executed by a corrupt judge. The grieving widow-mother then transforms into the title heroine and leads her followers into the rebel movement and executes the colonel of the federal troops in her region. THE MEXICAN REVOLUTIONISTS (1912) recounts the suspenseful odyssey of a rebel named Juan who is captured by the *federales* but escapes to help his fellow rebels capture Guadalajara.

Films about the Revolution while it was happening must have provided a vicarious thrill even to moviegoers largely ignorant about their southern neighbor. Alas, fair-minded and realistic Revolu-

tion-themed movies like the last two were far less popular or widely seen than, say, Tom Mix vehicles of the late teens like ALONG THE BORDER, AN ARIZONA WOOING and THE SHERIFF'S BLUNDER. All of them set forth the Yankee cowboy as a knight in shining armor (and in the first two he rescues a "golden heroine") who unmasks deceitful Mexican robbers posing as political insurrectionists.

Since all the rebels turn out to be crooks in disguise, the impression given American audiences was that the Mexican Revolution was less a spontaneous movement of the downtrodden than a violent masquerade by opportunistic Mexican bandits.

Hollywood has historically sided with right-wing governments against populist uprisings, whether in films about the French, Mexican or other non-American revolutions. In silent movies where the U.S. cavalry saved the day, bogus Mexican rebels were shown covering their tracks by informing the masses of their plans to depose the rich and enfranchise the poor. These sentiments were written to

(*Opposite page and above*) Dolores Del Rio: late-'20s glamour photography

alarm the same audiences who found nothing wrong with Robin Hood's credo of stealing from the rich to give to the poor. But, then, Robin Hood was very Anglo-Saxon!

For better and mostly for worse, Pancho Villa fascinated and infuriated Hollywood and its audiences. This daring agrarian revolutionary seized moviemakers' imaginations with his exploits and incursions into U.S. territory. Hollywood's Mutual Film Corporation felt that no movie could match the real thing, and so signed Villa to a contract (for $25,000) allowing Mutual to follow and record on camera his feats of derring-do. In return, his munitions-poor forces agreed to fight only during daylight hours and to hold off attacks until Mutual's cameras were in position. It was a peculiar case of Hollywood not only recording history but also altering it!

Villa took well to film, and signed a second contract, for a biographical feature to be helmed by D.W. Griffith. But because the director was too busy back home shooting BIRTH OF A NATION, another filmmaker was given charge of THE LIFE OF VILLA (1915), in which future director Raoul Walsh played Pancho as a youth. Again, Hollywood dwelt on the military side of the Revolution, rather than the political or philosophical differences between the two sides. *The New York Times* needlessly pointed out, "There are many scenes in which General Villa is seen directing the movements of his troops and artillery, and cavalry battles are shown with remarkable clearness. Other views show the burning of dead bodies on the battlefield."

When distorting or "documenting" the Revolution grew stale, it could be played for laughs, as in 1915's THE MEXICAN'S CHICKENS, whose protagonist is a poor chicken farmer named Señor Sourface. He joins the *federales* because the rebels are supposedly stealing his chickens. Captured by the rebels, he is punished by being shot out of a cannon. But it turns out that Sourface is an ex-circus performer, and in mid-flight he steers a new course and lands safely in a blanket being held by his wife and daughter a mile away from the man-spitting cannon!

Things hadn't improved by 1923, in THE BAD MAN, another full-length greaser comedy, although not labeled as such. The antagonist is one Pancho Lopez, a "brown buffoon" as ludicrous as he is menacing. Tweaking his mustache, Lopez brags

players. An example was THE MARK OF ZORRO (1920), a vehicle for Douglas Fairbanks, in the dual roles of Zorro and Don Diego Vega. Zorro had originated in a 1919 magazine serial; the story of a masked Robin Hood fighting corruption in Old California became an instant hit, whatever form it took. In 1925, Fairbanks made a sequel, DON Q, SON OF ZORRO.

Over the years, Zorro has been essayed by Tyrone Power (1940), George Hamilton (1981) and Frenchman Alain Delon in 1974. Zorro also inspired five or more Republic serials, a Walt Disney feature and TV series—starring Guy Williams, né Armando Catalano, the sole Hispanic to don the crusader's black cape—a 1974 telefilm with Frank

Hollywood newcomer Gilbert Roland

that he killed a Gringo for breakfast because "Heem call me dirty crook." For lunch, "I keel some more and steal ees pocketbook." *Olé?*

Most of these non-classics of the silent screen are now lost, if not missed. Obviously, most of the Hispanic actors employed in them didn't build lasting careers, for those mostly B-pictures seldom featured stars—except when the Yankee hero was incarnated by a Tom Mix. After sound came in, several unemployed actors with strong accents or who didn't speak English sought to return to Mexico or elsewhere, for work. They were often denied employment there because of their participation in Hollywood pictures that had demeaned their countrypeople.

Back in Hollywood, "high-class" Hispanic actors repeatedly found that big-budget movies with major Hispanic characters usually cast American

Langella, and even a 1970s porno spoof! Tyrone Power once called Zorro "the closest thing to a non-American version of Superman."

The diminutive but devastating Lupe Velez (née Maria Guadalupe Velez de Villalobos) made her screen debut in two 1927 shorts. The following year, she made the big-time opposite Douglas Fairbanks in THE GAUCHO. Improbably, Fairbanks (a Hungarian Jew, like Leslie Howard) played an Argentine cowboy, while the Mexican actress, dressed in white in a Spanish lace mantilla, undertook the first in a string of fire-spitting vamps. She confirmed her screen image in D.W. Griffith's LADY OF THE PAVEMENTS and in WOLF SONG (both 1929), opposite Gary Cooper in the latter.

Despite having been schooled in a convent in San Antonio, Texas, Velez (1908-1944) became even better known for her private life than her career, indulging in noisy and well-publicized affairs with actors like Cooper and John Gilbert before settling down to a tempestuous marriage to Johnny "Tarzan" Weissmuller. Though she became a star in the late '20s, the vocally expressive Velez didn't hit her stride until the Talking Thirties.

Donald Keith, Clara Bow and Gilbert Roland in THE PLASTIC AGE (1925)

Billie Dove and Gilbert Roland in THE LOVE MART (1927)

Asked the main difference between herself and rival Del Rio, Velez replied, "I don't know. But the *señoritas* I play seem to have more temperament. I don't know if this is good, but my audiences enjoy it!"

In 1927, Del Rio got to play the passionate title role in THE LOVES OF CARMEN, which cast Englishman Victor McLaglen as Escamillo (likewise, the 1948 remake cast Canadian Glenn Ford as Don Jose, and starred Rita Hayworth). Even the enduringly popular Cisco Kid began his screen life via a non-Hispanic actor. Warner Baxter played him thrice through 1939, and was critically the most successful actor in the part: in 1929, he won the second Best Actor Academy Award, for IN OLD ARIZONA, the first sound Western. The film co-starred Dorothy Burgess in historically incorrect brown-face as the Kid's mantilla-ed love interest.

The Cisco Kid's ethnic origins were deliberately clouded, but presumably Hispanic or Spanish. Post-Baxter, he was incarnated by mostly Hispanic actors, although a cinematic hero. This was progress, as even Baxter, best known as the Crime Doctor in Columbia's 1940s series, admitted. "It was high time (by the late '30s) that the Spanish-speaking peoples had a movie hero of their own, played by one of their own.

"I was delighted to play the part, and win the

Gilbert Roland and Norma Talmadge in CAMILLE (1927)

Douglas Fairbanks Sr. as DON Q., SON OF ZORRO (1925)

Antonio Moreno

Oscar. Who would say no to a good offer? But not only was I the wrong nationality to play Cisco Kid, I was the wrong age. If you recall, he was written as being about 25 but looking 20—that's why they called him 'Kid.' I wasn't the last actor who played him who was old enough to be his father . . ."

The cross-casting of American actors in Hispanic roles might not have finally been breached without individual and governmental Hispanic protests against stereotyping. Gradually, audiences got used to the idea of a Hispanic good guy, and even a Hispanic playing a major Hispanic role. Of course, the practice of cross-casting still continues—as recently and controversially as 1987's THE MILAGRO BEANFIELD WAR, directed by Robert Redford—despite the abundance of well-trained Hispanic actors of all physical descriptions.

For the most part, we've come a long way. But as Ramon Novarro put it in 1960, "The age of the 'greaser' is finally past, thank goodness." The actor had just completed a small role in his final film, George Cukor's HELLER IN PINK TIGHTS. "In the old days, whenever they could, they used our skin color against us. Today, they use our accents . . ."

Billie Dove and Antonio Moreno in CAREERS (1929)

Warner Baxter and Dorothy Burgess in IN OLD ARIZONA

Antonio Moreno and Clara Bow in IT (1927)

Greta Garbo and Antonio Moreno in THE TEMPTRESS (1926)

Gary Cooper and Lupe Velez,
more than friends

Raquel Torres enjoyed Hollywood popularity in the late-
'20s and early-'30s

Gilbert Roland and Dolores Del Rio at the premiere of JUAREZ

2. THE THIRTIES:
Glamour & Grit

"During the first few decades of talkies, if you spoke Spanish, or if your parents did, you were treated as local color and stuck behind a boulder or inside a barroom."
— Antonio Moreno in *In View*, 1957

The sound era in Latin America began unofficially on July 6, 1929, when THE JAZZ SINGER starring Al Jolson opened at Mexico City's Olimpia Theatre. Two years later came the first Mexican talkie, SANTA, a remake of a 1918 silent. The picture was directed by Antonio Moreno, by then past the silent glory in which he'd emoted opposite Garbo, Gish, Mary Pickford, Gloria Swanson, Clara Bow and others.

From Hollywood, SANTA also imported Lupita Tovar, to co-star in what *Todo* magazine called "the three-hankie saga of a country girl's misadventures in the big city." The leading man, likewise from Hollywood, was Donald Reed, who took the stage name Ernesto Guillen. With its subtheme of prostitution, the film was a hit, and in 1932, Moreno

helmed one more, AGUILAS FRENTE AL SOL (*Eagles Facing the Sun*).

He then did some Mexican films as an actor before returning to higher-paying Hollywood as he grew accustomed to smaller roles. He later told a Mexican reporter, "By the late '30s, I was in Hollywood again. By then I was in my fifties, so my roles in movies like TWO LATINS FROM MANHATTAN, THEY MET IN ARGENTINA and FIESTA or TAMPICO were rather small. Fortunately, I had years to get down from Mount Olympus . . ."

Ramon Novarro had a classy shot at talkie stardom: 1931's MATA HARI, co-starring Greta Garbo. Contrary to rumor, his voice—like John Gilbert's—was not high-pitched, nor did he ever utter the line, "What's the matter, Mata?" Rather, Novarro's

51

Lupita Tovar, star of Mexico's first talkie, SANTA (1931)

language versions of its movies for export—i.e., Garbo's first talkie, ANNA CHRISTIE, was also filmed in French and German.) But by 1933, Roland's accent reduced him to supporting roles; in the Gay '90s classic SHE DONE HIM WRONG, he played a Russian gigolo described by Mae West as "warm, dark and handsome."

Roland too appeared in Spanish-language movies, like the 1933 YO, TU Y ELLA (*I, You and She*) and the 1935 JULIETA COMPRA UN HIJO (*Juliet Buys a Son*). The burgeoning movie industries in Mexico, Argentina and Spain beckoned to Spanish-speaking actors still able to command leading roles outside Hollywood. Through the silent era, Latin American filmmakers had been unable to effectively compete with Hollywood's product, a situation altered overnight by talkies. In Lillian Gish's words, "Before they put in speech, our pictures were for a *world* audience, and everybody could share them."

Gilbert Roland

film career was largely undone by his refusing Louis B. Mayer's ultimatum that he marry, in order to conceal his homosexuality, (Antonio Moreno had concealed his in his late thirties).

Novarro too turned to directing, first in 1930 with LA SEVILLANA, the Hollywood Spanish-language version of CALL OF THE FLESH—he also starred in the English, Spanish and French versions. In 1936, in Mexico, he helmed, produced and wrote CONTRA LA CORRIENTE (*Against the Current*), then the next year took up where Valentino had left off, in THE SHEIK STEPS OUT. By the late 1930s, he was undertaking screen work in France and elsewhere, before returning to Hollywood films in 1949. "When Hollywood chooses to forget you," he remarked, "they forget very fast." Old-timers still remembered Novarro in the 1950s, and on I LOVE LUCY, he was mentioned as the favorite star of Lucy's mother and her elderly neighbor.

Meanwhile, in 1930, Gilbert Roland starred in MEN OF THE NORTH and its Spanish-language version. (Hollywood was experimenting with foreign-

Gilbert Roland and Rosita Ballesteros in MONSIEUR LE FOX, the Spanish version of MEN OF THE NORTH (1930)

The Spanish Civil War drastically reduced Spain's filmic output, with the gap mostly filled by Mexican and Argentine pictures. Mexico invited Dolores Del Rio to make a movie there, but she declined, opining that Mexican films weren't yet "of sufficient solidity." This somewhat alienated her from her countrypeople, and she resisted Mexican films until 1943. Nor was her image among Hispanics aided by the fact that all her Hollywood publicity billed her as "a Spanish actress."

However, like Lupe Velez, Del Rio fared better in talkies than her male counterparts. As already noted, an accent was considered more acceptable, and even glamorous, in an actress. The former "Female Valentino" had a huge hit with 1932's BIRD OF PARADISE, as a near-topless Polynesian in leis and love with Joel McCrea. Another Mexican

actress who played Polynesian was Movita (Movita Luisa Castaneda) in the 1935 MUTINY ON THE BOUNTY starring Clark Gable as Fletcher Christian. Errol Flynn played the role in an Australian film (IN THE WAKE OF THE BOUNTY, 1933), and later renamed his Dutch-Mexican discovery Linda Christian—she'd been born Blanca Rosa Welter in Tampico, Mexico. Del Rio followed up with THE GIRL OF THE RIO (1932) and FLYING DOWN TO RIO (1933). The latter made stars of Fred Astaire and Ginger Rogers—supporting actors, at the time— but created a sensation when Del Rio, playing a Brazilian, introduced the two-piece swimsuit.

There were more hits, among them WONDER BAR and the title role in MADAME DUBARRY, both 1934. Yet, later in the decade her star plummeted, with projects like INTERNATIONAL SETTLEMENT (1938). "By the mid-1930s," she explained, "there was a new set of fresh faces, and the really plum roles were going to actresses like Bette Davis or Katharine Hepburn or Barbara Stanwyck." At last, Del Rio departed for Mexico, where Zuñiga promptly sculpted her and Rivera painted her.

Post-silents, Lupe Velez was discovered to have a voice alternately husky and cartoon-like; as she once admitted, "Sometimes I sound just like Donald *Duke*." With the Depression's dampening of enthusiasm for foreign stars, Velez now found

Gilbert Roland and Mae West in SHE DONE HIM WRONG (1933)

Gilbert Roland and Catalina Borcena in JULIETA COMPRA UN HIJO (Juliet Buys a Son, 1936)

her roles skimpier. In the 1931 remake of the classic THE SQUAW MAN, as a Native American she "does little but look dejected," and in KONGO (1932), she looks anguished while, as Walter Huston's mistress, he twists her tongue with a wire during the torture of her lover, who is immersed up to his neck in a swamp.

"I never seem to play nobody normal," Velez understated in *Photoplay*.

The value of her '30s pictures can be guessed at by such titles as HOT PEPPER (1933), STRICTLY DYNAMITE (1934) and THE MORALS OF MARCUS (1935). Fed up, Velez in 1937 went to Mexico to film the love story LA ZANDUNGA for Fernando de Fuentes. It wasn't the hoped-for hit, but in 1939 Lupe's career was rocketed by THE GIRL FROM MEXICO. As Carmelita Fuentes, she energetically launched the Mexican Spitfire series. Through eight films, she was a veritable one-woman equivalent of the Three Stooges—yelling, punching, kicking and throwing, as well as mangling English in a way that prefigured Carmen Miranda and Charo (both born in Europe but identified as Latinas).

The Mexican Revolution was long past by the '30s. Ditto Pancho Villa, the sole Hispanic figure to grab Hollywood's attention for any length of time.

With sound, Mexican-themed pictures and characters gradually became rarer, even in Westerns. The biggest reason was the Depression, which sparked greater concern with America's own problems and produced a larger percentage of fantasy musicals and escapist films about the idle rich.

The massive flow of immigration had by then been stopped in its tracks, and as Europe slid steadily toward war, America asserted its isolationist stance. Hollywood concentrated on the American heritage, churning out films about Lincoln, the Civil War, the Western pioneers, the Dust Bowl and the rise of Chicago's gangsters. Films also showcased actresses as that post-'20s American phenomenon, the "career girl." Little room was made in such pictures for Hispanic characters.

But now that English-language talkies had a shrunken share of Latin American and Spanish markets, Hollywood began to make its own Spanish-language films (even though French, German and Italian versions were soon dropped). Out of necessity, Hollywood made over 110 movies in Spanish between 1930 and 1938; films with Spanish subtitles had proven impractical because of Latin America's high illiteracy rate.

Predictably, most of Hollywood's prestigious Hispanic stars didn't appear in its non-English films. Del Rio and Velez, for instance, made their Spanish-language films outside the U.S., although Ramon Novarro did participate in a few of Hollywood's Spanish talkies.

Unpredictably, these movies failed in overseas markets *and* among Hispanic moviegoers in the U.S. The reason was linguistic. Or dialectical. The melange of accents—Mexican, Spanish, Cuban, Chilean, Argentine—made the Hollywood hybrids unreal and unacceptable to audiences in Latin America.

In Spain, the situation was worse. Spanish critics considered the verbal mishmash a profanation of classical Castilian, and the government informed Hollywood that Spaniards couldn't "bear to listen to the irritating Latin American accents." Furthermore, if the "c" or "z" were not "orthographically pronounced," the Hollywood studios "need not bother" sending their output to Spanish cinemas!

Spanish-speaking audiences in the U.S. couldn't accept Hollywood's substitution of glamorous superstars with Spanish-fluent players like Jose Crespo or Luana Alcañiz. American luminaries like

BIRD OF PARADISE

The grandest romance ever written . . . most famous of all American plays sweeps to the screen a flaming pageant of a forbidden love. White man . . . brown girl . . . caught in the volcanic drama of life . . . on the moon drenched shores of a magic isle . . . where blood runs hot and the heart is free and man holds in fierce embrace the alluring image of elemental woman as the jealous God in the Mountain of Fire sunders the earth and splits the skies and hurls the sea to a bottomless pit because she broke the savage Taboo!

The "daring" BIRD OF PARADISE (1932) starred Dolores Del Rio and Joel McCrea

55

Greta Garbo and Ramon Novarro in MATA HARI (1932)

Joan Crawford and Clark Gable couldn't speak other languages, while the Europeans—Garbo, Dietrich, Boyer, Chevalier—were typically multilingual, but not including Spanish.

Thus, by decade's end, Hollywood's Spanish-language efforts had expired from audience neglect and stars' inability or disdain. Dolores Del Rio admitted in the '70s that "For those of us in A-pictures, it would have been unwise to do 'foreign' pictures with the same production values as B-movies." Ironically, at the time of Del Rio's silent triumphs, she spoke no English. She had to learn it after sound came in.

1933 saw the screen debut of ex-dancer Cesar Romero (born 1907), a descendant of Cuban liberator José Martí. After co-starring in von Sternberg and Dietrich's 1935 THE DEVIL IS A WOMAN, Romero alternated American and ethnic roles, in films like PUBLIC ENEMY'S WIFE (1936), Shirley Temple's WEE WILLIE WINKIE (1937) and CHARLIE CHAN AT TREASURE ISLAND (1939). Romero's screen heyday would arrive in the 1940s, when he would enrich the Latinate Fox musicals featuring that Lady in the Tutti-Frutti Hat, Carmen Miranda. His movie career had its ups and downs, but his fame revived in the 1960s via TV, as Batman's nemesis, the Joker, and in the '80s via his Greek billionaire role on FALCON CREST. Also, to his credit, the entirely American-sounding Romero didn't change his name and has always proclaimed his Hispanic heritage.

In 1939, Romero had a supporting role in RETURN OF THE CISCO KID (he assumed the title role the following year). This was the third entry starring Warner Baxter, who in 1936 was Hollywood's top-paid actor. In 1931, Baxter had made THE CISCO KID. "Looking back," he said, "it's surprising no one thought of starring the Cisco Kid more often. I know that the studio got a lot of fan mail from people with Spanish last names, praising the character, and average audiences took a shine to him.

"But once they got him going, as a series, in the '40s, he really took off, and I don't think there's been a more positive role model of his sort." More about the Kid later.

In 1936, Baxter starred as ROBIN HOOD OF EL DORADO, a popular escapist adventure that blended legend and reality. Joaquin Murieta was a real-life bandit-hero in Early California who stole from the

Screen newcomer Cesar Romero

Dolores Del Rio starred in the controversial GIRL OF THE RIO (1932) and its notorious sequel IN CALIENTE (1935)

rich and frequently corrupt, and gave to the poor. El Dorado, of course, was the myth of the Midas-like gilded king who so inflamed the Spanish conquistadores' gold-lust. To his disenfranchised beneficiaries, Murieta must have seemed an El Dorado himself. His story long outlived him, and today he is commemorated in several California place names.

In 1965, blue-eyed sex symbol Jeffrey Hunter played Murieta in MURIETA; in Great Britain, where Murieta is all but unknown, the film was titled VENDETTA. Ricardo Montalban also essayed the Murieta role in the 1971 made-for-television movie THE DESPERATE MISSION.

Well into the Depression, 1934 newcomer Rita Cansino (neé Margarita Carmen Cansino) didn't get anywhere fast via *her* original moniker. Her first dozen films numbered UNDER THE PAMPAS MOON, 1935 (starring Warner Baxter as disillusioned gaucho Cesar Campo), CHARLIE CHAN IN EGYPT, 1935 (with Swedish Warner Oland as the Chinese detective) and HUMAN CARGO, 1936, wherein Rita played an illegal alien named Carmen Zoro.

Warner Baxter told the Hollywood foreign press, "This is Señorita Cansino's first important picture

. . . I predict she will make her mark as a dancer. In this picture, we introduce a dance called the Zamba, which Rita practiced with her father, who is a dance expert. She has few lines, but when she dances, she is brilliantly alive."

When Cansino asked the film's dialogue director "what kind of accent we were supposed to simulate for our characters, he said, 'Standard Hollywood-Mexican—nobody will know the difference!'" She added that almost nobody saw the picture, and Baxter noted that interest in Hispanic-themed films was waning: "With so much going on in Europe now, movies are starting to look eastward, rather than southward."

In 1937, the dancer-actress began her ascent to the dazzling stardom of Rita Hayworth (1918-1987). She later explained, "After I changed my name, the quality of roles offered to me improved greatly." Another contributing factor to her fame was the switch from brunette to redhead.

Pedro Armendáriz (1912-1963) also came to the screen in 1934, and quickly became a staple of Mexican cinema. Despite a Hollywood fling in the late '40s, his English-speaking career was undistinguished—and apparently fatal, for he died of can-

cer probably contracted on the radioactive Nevada locations for THE CONQUEROR, John Wayne's 1956 Mongol epic. Armendáriz is best known to Americans for his last film, the second 007 entry, FROM RUSSIA WITH LOVE (1963), in which he was a Turk.

Not long after, he shot himself to death while suffering from the inoperable cancer.

One-quarter Irish, Anthony Rudolph Oaxaca Quinn (born 1915) hailed from Chihuahua, Mexico, where his grandmother was "a great movie fan who loved Antonio Moreno and Ramon Novarro. She made me promise to get into the movies." At four, Quinn was transplanted to Hollywood, where his father became an assistant cameraman and Valentino "wanted to adopt me."

In 1936, Quinn debuted in speaking roles with a 45-second part in PAROLE! It was to be a long haul before stardom, for Quinn's self-described "Aztec face" worked against him, professionally and

Ricardo Cortez ropes
Dolores Del Rio in
WONDER BAR (1934)

socially (he was initially shunned by his father-in-law, Cecil B. DeMille). In between assignments as Latinos and "Indians," he played Chinese, Arabs, Greeks, Rumanians, an Eskimo(!) and even Attila the Hun. He also co-starred in several pictures with Hollywood's sole Oriental star, Anna May Wong. Not until the 1950s would he receive three-dimensional roles commensurate with his talent.

The first notes of Xavier Cugat's 30-year screen career were heard in 1930. With his band of Latino musicians, the "Rhumba King" played himself (born Jan. 1, 1900) and invigorated such films as GO WEST, YOUNG MAN (1936) and THE HEAT'S ON (1943), both starring Mae West. In the mid-'40s, he moved to MGM until 1949, when the craze for Latin rhythms had petered out.

As they created their own stars, Latin American film industries were better able to compete with Hollywood in Spanish-speaking markets inside and outside the U.S. In 1936, Mexico introduced Mario Moreno (born 1911) in NO TE ENGAÑES, CORAZÓN (*Don't Fool Yourself, Heart*). As Cantinflas, he would be known as "the Mexican Charlie Chaplin" before going on to conquer Spanish-language box

offices on three continents. His two Hollywood turns amounted to glorified servant roles (e.g., AROUND THE WORLD IN 80 DAYS, 1956, starring David Niven).

But even without Hollywood, Cantinflas eventually became the 20th century's biggest movie star in the Spanish language.

Stereotypes were not gone by the 1930s, but they were less frequent and less vicious. As the power of cinema became more obvious, governments sought to become more involved. In the '30s, Mexican and other governments stepped up their protests to Hollywood; President Lazaro Cardenas, who nationalized Mexico's oil industry in 1938, was especially vocal. Films with particularly offensive anti-Hispanic material were now banned in most Latin countries. Partly in response, Franklin Roosevelt formulated the Good Neighbor Policy which saw fruition in the '40s.

In 1934, with the help of religious groups and the tacit approval of the U.S. government, Joseph I. Breen, director (since 1931) of the Code Administration, instigated a puritanical movie censorship

60

Dolores Del Rio, brunette and blonde, in MADAME DUBARRY (1934)

code which lasted, unchallenged, until the mid-1950s. Among other characters banished from the screen were vamps and prostitutes. Thus, the "dark lady," or Latina of easy virtue, was a thing of the past, and had to be performed—comic-chastely—for laughs, in the Lupe Velez manner. Screen Latinas were now less sexy; they were also becoming funnier and more frivolous.

If the scalding Lupe was fire, Dolores Del Rio was ice, and in 1932, she starred in THE GIRL OF THE RIO. The hit film angered and activated Hispanics and drew a formal protest from the Mexican government for its depiction of Mexican justice as "a reflection of who could pay the most for the verdict of their liking." In it, Leo Carrillo (1880-1961) played a crypto-greaser named Señor Tostado (Mr. Toast), out to assault a cantina dancer called The Dove (Del Rio) who is already engaged to an American gambler named Johnny Powell (Norman Foster, later a director, then wed to Claudette Colbert).

Tostado manages to frame the easygoing Yankee

Dolores Del Rio and George Sanders in LANCER SPY (1937)

for a murder he himself has committed, but unavoidably comes to a richly deserved end. *Motion Picture Herald* called THE GIRL OF THE RIO "suspenseful entertainment, with a gleefully loathesome villain!" What made the picture more repellent was its success with mainstream audiences. RIO was banned in Mexico, and Panama and Nicaragua did likewise, prompting Spain and several Latin American countries to enact reciprocal treaties banning films which "attacked, slandered, defamed, insulted or misrepresented" peoples of Hispanic or Spanish origin.

Repeated offenses would incur a ban of all movies produced by an offending studio. The readiness of nations like Peru, Chile, Argentina, El Salvador, plus those mentioned above, to participate in Mexico's boycott reflected the undeniable fact that Hollywood's "Mexican" was a universal Hispanic stereotype without national boundaries.

But protests or no, THE GIRL OF THE RIO spawned, IN CALIENTE (1935), with the same cast.

The portly Carrillo appeared in forgettable '30s fare like MOONLIGHT AND PRETZELS, RACETRACK, ARIZONA WILDCAT, GIRL OF THE GOLDEN WEST and THE CHICKEN WAGON FAMILY. Best known as the Cisco Kid's sidekick Pancho in the '40s series star-

Ramon Novarro and Jeanette MacDonald in THE CAT AND THE FIDDLE (1934)

ring Duncan Renaldo, Carrillo, according to writer Gary D. Keller, "lived down to the stereotype faithfully, as a gambling, murdering, extorting, pimping, (usually) border bandit in 25 or 30 films."

Actually, Carrillo made over 30 movies during the 1930s, and in almost half he played characters embroiled in illegal activities, typically gambling and/or murder. According to Rutgers history professor Allen Woll, "Even if Carrillo had a legitimate source of money, as in GIRL OF THE RIO or in IN CALIENTE, he still was depicted as bearing an uncontrollable urge to engage in illegal acts." And gambling was often associated with screen Latinos, especially self-made ones, just as 1970s films would often portray a wealthy black male as a pimp.

Carrillo also appeared in some of the so-called "greaser-gangsters," a sub-genre of the gangster

Ramon Novarro followed in Valentino's footsteps in THE SHEIK STEPS OUT (1937)

Lupe Velez in HE LOVED AN ACTRESS (1937)

flicks which became so popular in the early '30s and made stars of Cagney, Bogart, George Raft and Edward G. Robinson. Another dubious film specimen was the "Three Mesquiteers" series, featuring Anglo cowboy trios among the mesquite and the Chicano stereotypes. Rita Cansino played the token dancing señorita in one of these B-minus pictures, HIT THE SADDLE (1937):

"I don't know why they bothered putting me in the picture, which was full of action and stunts and even a Western ventriloquist and his dummy!"

The Three Mesquiteers made their screen bow in 1935 in POWDERSMOKE RANGE, via RKO. The cowboy triumvirate—one was the romantic, one the brawn, one the comic—was drawn from the novels of William Colt MacDonald. In 1936, the newly formed Republic Pictures took over the series, and in 15 films the leads were played by Robert Living-

ston, Ray "Crash" Corrigan and Max Terhune. Eventual co-stars included John Wayne and Duncan Renaldo. In all, there were 52 of the shortish but fast-paced and action-packed movies. The last one, in 1943, was RIDERS OF THE RIO GRANDE.

Renaldo, later better known as the Cisco Kid, once commented, "I don't think that series was unusually harmful or derogatory, but it did reinforce the idea that the non-Americans of the Southwest were rather helpless or incompetent . . . I was glad for the change, once the Kid came along."

The 1934 MGM production VIVA VILLA! created a commotion *before* its completion. Makeup man Frank Westmore recalled that the film's stars, Wallace Beery and Lee Tracy, would habitually get drunk on location in Mexico. "One night during a fiesta taking place beneath the balcony of their

Lupe Velez as MEXICAN SPITFIRE (1939)

hotel suite, Tracy stepped out on the balcony and serenely and copiously peed on the crowd below, nearly starting a revolution."

The incident inspired a famous telegram sent by *Time* magazine's correspondent to his New York office: TRACY NUDE, LEWD, RUDE, STEWED, AND PEED ON PARADE. Tracy was also fired, replaced by actor Stuart Erwin.

VV's original director was Howard Hawks, who halfway through filming was summoned back to the U.S. to bear witness against Lee Tracy, who'd "allegedly made insulting remarks about the Mexican army" during the film's shooting. Appalled by both Tracy's unprofessional behavior (with its resultant bad publicity) and the "nuisance complaints," as he described them, Hawks left the project and was replaced by Jack Conway, who shot most of VV's interiors, in Hollywood.

Hollywood in the Thirties author John Baxter felt that the picture "has a power not often encountered in action melodramas of the time. It is a strange poem of violence; ragged groups of cavalry surge out of dust clouds like avenging ghosts or stand impassive around a doomed man; a murder is suggested by the movement of a boy out of a lighted door into a shadowed street to follow the footsteps of his victim; in a final sequence, at the climax of his victory, the bandit strips and flogs a beautiful aristocrat in a frenzied mutilation of that which he is brutishly unable to make his own."

Written by Ben Hecht and produced by David O. Selznick, VIVA VILLA! received Oscar nominations for Best Screenplay and Film. But despite its rare location footage and the fact that it was the first Hollywood script submitted for approval to the Mexican government, VILLA's Villa left much to be

desired. According to *Motion Picture*, "Beery's is a caricature amounting to equal parts booze, buffoonery, lechery and murder."

Another critic felt the "overtly fictionalized account" made Villa "a cross between Robin Hood and the Marquis de Sade." *Reel Politics* author Terry Christensen found the film's messages mixed. "It supported revolution—at least in Mexico—but disapproved of revolutionaries . . . A few rich liberals seemed nice but ineffective. In the end, VIVA VILLA! seemed to say that Villa and (Francisco) Madero were unsuccessful."

However, it represented progress that an A-picture had tackled a purely Hispanic subject.

A year later came the first Hispanic social problem film, Warner Bros.' BORDERTOWN, starring Paul Muni as Johnny Ramirez, a hardworking young law student and then lawyer. The story begins straightforwardly enough, and illustrates the problems facing an upwardly mobile Hispanic. Muni played Ramirez without Beeryesque stereotyping, but BORDERTOWN is basically a melodrama-cum-thriller, and Muni is inescapably an actor in brownface.

Nor were the stereotypes completely absent, for one is asked to believe that after several years of

(*Here, and facing page*) Glamour queen Lupe Velez

67

Arturo De Cordova (here with Joaquín Pardavé) in QUE VIENE MI MARIDO (My Husband's Coming, 1939)

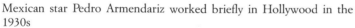

Mexican star Pedro Armendariz worked briefly in Hollywood in the 1930s

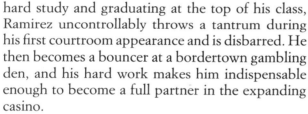

hard study and graduating at the top of his class, Ramirez uncontrollably throws a tantrum during his first courtroom appearance and is disbarred. He then becomes a bouncer at a bordertown gambling den, and his hard work makes him indispensable enough to become a full partner in the expanding casino.

The "color issue" is brought home when Ramirez falls for a society lady (Margaret Lindsay) who proves unattainable. He next shifts his attentions to the very attainable wife of the casino owner (Bette Davis), who kills her husband (Eugene Pallette) so she can be with Ramirez full-time. When he learns of the murder, he spurns her; she tries to implicate him, and the police arrest both and bring them to trial. In the courtroom, the widow cracks up—in what Gary Keller deemed "Bette Davis' standard performance as a lunatic"—and Ramirez is acquitted.

Back at the casino, he again meets up with the heiress. He takes her for a drive, proposes marriage, and she retorts, "We aren't of the same tribe, sav-

Mexican sex symbol Arturo De Cordova

Mayhem in Gene Autry's GUNS AND GUITARS (1936; note the man as a woman, the WASP as an Indian and the black as an Oriental!)

age!" Ramirez becomes furious, for he thought she had mellowed toward him: "I was okay to kiss and have fun with, but not okay to marry." Frightened, the heiress bolts the car and, running across the road, is struck by another car and killed.

A remorseful Johnny Ramirez sells his interest in the casino and uses the money to found a law school in his hometown. He confesses to his priest that he will "Come back and live among my own people where I belong." He is alone now—despite a profusion of *Hispanic* women—and back in the barrio where he started.

Film Comment accused BORDERTOWN of "undercutting its reputation for progressivism with its downbeat finale, which implies that success isn't really desirable or even possible for a Johnny Ramirez."

The highly-regarded Muni's research method also seemed somewhat facile: he roamed Olvera Street in downtown Los Angeles, then decided that in order to convincingly enact a Mexican, "I have to go swimming in tequila," and so headed for Mexicali with Carroll Graham, author of the novel *Bordertown*. Muni did take Spanish lessons, to aid his accent.

Warners star Paul Muni played Mexican in BORDERTOWN (1935) and JUAREZ (1939)

If Latino subjects were rare in the mid- to late-'30s, rarer still were Latinos as Latinos. More common was a film like THE BOLD CABALLERO (1936), with Robert Livingston as a swordsman opposing a cruel California honcho played by Sig Rumann, and Heather Angel as the romantic interest. Typically, this minor but lively version of THE MARK OF ZORRO was reviewed solely for its action quotient and "lovely costumes."

In 1935, Lupe Velez told *Photoplay*, "When they review my pictures, they review a carnival act. They write how funny I am, not about who I am playing . . . This goes for any picture that goes a little south of the border! They don't take those pictures seriously, or *us* seriously." Neither did *Photoplay*, which ran Velez's quotes thus: ". . . Dey don't take doze peectures serioosly . . ."

If the Depression started to raise consciousnesses, it was lopsidedly, so far as screen Hispanics went. The "positive" trend in late-'30s films was the Anglo hero as Good Neighbor who rescues innocent, helpless Hispanics from their corrupt and lawless countrymen. Such was the case in programmers like ROSE OF THE RANCHO (1936), DURANGO VALLEY RAIDERS (1938), BORDER G-MAN (1938), plus Gene Autry, Roy Rogers, Tex Ritter, Lone Ranger and Hopalong Cassidy vehicles like SONG OF THE GRINGO (1936), IN OLD MEXICO (1938), SOUTH OF THE BORDER (1939), ad infinitum.

(To most Americans, the difference between Native Americans and mestizos was nil, and so the Lone Ranger's "Indian" sidekick was given the name of Stupid—*Tonto*, in Spanish.)

The underlying message in such Anglo-succors-Hispanic pictures was that Latins cannot help themselves. The Yankee must serve as an honorary Big Brother and inspiration. This reasoning infiltrated Warner Bros.' prestigious JUAREZ (1939), which starred Paul Muni as the hallowed Mexican President Benito Juarez. Again, Muni declaimed in brown-face, and Bette Davis portrayed a white woman who goes mad—Empress Carlotta, wife of the puppet-Emperor Maximilian (Brian Aherne) who was foisted on Mexico by Napoleon III (Claude Rains).

Not surprisingly, the film was a bigger hit in Latin America and Europe than in the U.S., despite the box office power of la Davis. The queen of the

(*Here, and on facing page*)
Paul Muni and Bette Davis in
BORDERTOWN

Margo made an impact in LOST HORIZON (1937), starring Ronald Colman (and John Howard, above, and Jane Wyatt, below)

Warners lot didn't receive top-billing because she wasn't portraying Juarez; by then, Muni had it in his contract that he got first place when performing a historical character, and that such a film's name had to be the same as his character's (Warners had wanted another title, because JUAREZ had "low recognition value").

The studio spent a near-record amount promoting the costly movie and devising print-worthy publicity stunts. One involved a publicist who ordered an East Coast taxi driver to "Take me to JUAREZ." They went all the way to Juarez, Mexico, and the resultant headline exclaimed, "Moviegoer Drives 2,500 Miles to See 'Juarez'!"

Paul Muni as Benito JUAREZ

Hollywood newcomer Anthony Quinn played a Spanish officer along with fellow hispanic Gilbert Roland and pseudo Latina Dorothy Lamour in THE LAST TRAIN FROM MADRID (1937)

Dolores Del Rio with Marlene Dietrich, Jean Harlow, Joan Blondell and Edward G. Robinson

In Mexico, JUAREZ was seen as the first tangible result of the Good Neighbor Policy, and the film was much honored. It was the first to be premiered in Mexico City's Palacio de Bellas Artes (Palace of Fine Arts), and the local media proudly declared that part of the movie's dialogue was lifted from Mexican Congressional debates of the period. With all its flaws, JUAREZ was nonetheless the most sincere, if ambivalent, effort Hollywood had made to realistically transmit the heritage of one of its Hispanic neighbors.

The film's split personality arises from its conflicting viewpoints and loyalties. Napoleon III is the villain, and his monarchial machinations are strongly resisted by Juarez and Porfirio Diaz (played by John Garfield). The struggle for native

Paul Muni as JUAREZ (1939)

Mexican singer José Mojica made Spanish-language talkies in Hollywood in the early 1930s

Bette Davis as Mexico's Empress Carlota (sic) in JUAREZ

democracy is riveting, but then the focus shifts to Carlotta and Maximilian, whose hearts are with the Mexicans but who are powerless to help their unwilling subjects.

One reviewer felt that Muni portrayed "the Mexican president as an extension of American democratic ideals and as a disciple of Abraham Lincoln." According to a *Los Angeles Times* unused to positive portraits of Hispanics, "JUAREZ continues the trend of gritty realism in motion pictures about our neighbor to the south. Nevertheless, the title character seems wooden and remote, as he is treated with much over-reverence."

Juarez indeed seems somewhat remote within his own biofilm, for although Napoleon III is the villain of the piece, Benito Juarez is not the hero. The hero is the United States, which for once supposedly intervenes to help a Latin neighbor. A saintly, omnipresent Abraham Lincoln is JUAREZ's real hero, and he is touchingly invoked by Juarez and Mexico—even though he was dead by the time America came to the celluloid rescue.

Ricardo Cortez as Sam Spade in THE MALTESE FALCON (1931)

Warner Baxter as the Cisco Kid (with Edmund Lowe) in
RETURN OF THE CISCO KID (1939)

Paul Muni and Bette Davis in BORDERTOWN (1935)

Dolores Del Rio, Spanish-style

Marlene Dietrich and Cesar Romero in THE DEVIL IS A WOMAN
(1935)

Paul Muni as JUAREZ

Rita Hayworth as GILDA (1946)

3. THE FORTIES:
Good Neighbors?

"Een Holleewood where I joos make two peecture, dey geev me some songs I should seeng in Eenglish. So I stoddy very hard and seeng in good Eenglish. Den wot? Dey holler at me and tell me to seeng in Souse American, like I talk! Dey must be notts!"
—Carmen Miranda in *Modern Screen*, 1941

Carmen Miranda (1909-1955) was the most famous Latin ever to grace a Hollywood film. The prototypical screen Latina, the "Brazilian Bombshell" was born in Portugal but mistaken by moviegoers for a generic Souse American. Her image was a Pan-American potpourri of fruits, colors, hips, pop-eyes and fractured Eenglish. But she was less a representative of a given country or culture than a unique autofact—one could sit up all night, imagination on full-throttle, and still not dream up someone like Carmen Miranda!

Her box office popularity, if relatively brief, and her prominence in Fox's jubilant 1940s musicals were a result of America's Good Neighbor Policy. During World War II, the policy sought to open up Latin markets for American culture and products (the war cut off European markets) and to pull Latin America more firmly into the U.S.' sphere of influence.

Another policy result was the popularity of Latin music. In the early '40s, its chief beneficiaries were Miranda and Cugat. Another was Andy Russell (né Andy Rabajos), who sang solos and duets in various '40s musicals but ended his screen career in 1947's COPACABANA, starring Carmen Miranda and Groucho Marx. Ironically, it was about a Latina singer whose agent (Marx) can't get her work, because the Latin craze has faded (the agent's solution is to disguise Carmen Navarro as Mademoiselle Fifi, a French chanteuse [editorial note: Navarro is the Portuguese form of Novarro]).

Post-Hollywood, Russell moved to Argentina,

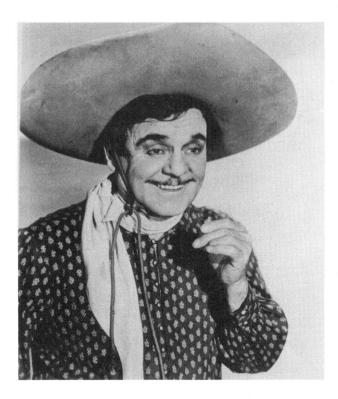

Leo Carrillo as Pancho, the Cisco Kid's sidekick

where his singing career thrived. In the 1970s, his rendition of "Love Story" went to No. 1 on local hit parades.

1942 saw two comely Latinas' screen debuts. Acquanetta was neither a swimming star nor a hairspray model, but the "Venezuelan Volcano," an actress of exotic beauty but limited ability. Née

Burnu Acquanetta (born 1921) and hailing from Wyoming, she was discovered by Charles Boyer and first appeared in ARABIAN NIGHTS (1942), a Maria Montez vehicle. Following this, she was seen opposite Lon Chaney, Jr., in DEAD MAN'S EYES and in CAPTIVE WILD WOMAN, which actually warranted a sequel, JUNGLE WOMAN. Acquanetta's feral image was reinforced by TARZAN AND THE LEOPARD WOMAN (1946), before stereotyping strangled her career.

Lina (née Elena) Romay (born 1922) was billed as "Cugie's Latin Doll" and sang with the bandleader for two years. As part of his act, she made her screen bow in YOU WERE NEVER LOVELIER (1942), a Rita Hayworth vehicle. After leaving the band—it was Cugat who changed her first name—she found solo stardom via an MGM contract, which she signed in 1944, appearing in singing numbers in films like WEEKEND AT THE WALDORF (1945) and LOVE LAUGHS AT ANDY HARDY (1946), and doing a straight role in the Clark Gable vehicle ADVENTURE (1945). In the latter, she played Maria, the daughter of a Chilean diplomat; in real life, Lina was the Brooklyn-born daughter of a Mexican diplomat.

Another Latin from Manhattan (or Brooklyn, anyway) was Olga San Juan (born 1927), a "triple threat" singer-dancer-actress billed as "The Puerto Rican Pepperpot." She bowed in RAINBOW ISLAND (1944), then trilled to audiences in DUFFY'S TAVERN (1945), BLUE SKIES (1946), VARIETY GIRL (1947) and ONE TOUCH OF VENUS (1948). Like all the musical Hispanic performers, San Juan found that changing tastes—specifically the end of WWII and the slow death of the Good Neighbor Policy—spelled an end to a once-flourishing career. (She married actor Edmond O'Brien, and had a fling on Broadway as the female lead in *Paint Your Wagon*. Their daughter Maria now is an actress in TV movies). Only Carmen Miranda, who'd best symbolized the period's energy, managed to hold out till the mid-'50s.

Another beneficiary of '40s *salsa*—also the conga, rhumba and samba—was Cesar Romero, who didn't sing but danced in such hits as WEEKEND IN HAVANA (1941), SPRINGTIME IN THE ROCKIES (1942) and CARNIVAL IN COSTA RICA (1947). The Mexican actress Margo (wife of Eddie Albert and mother of Edward Albert) is best remembered for her non-dancing role in LOST

HORIZON (1937) and for THE LEOPARD MAN (1943), in which she played Clo-Clo, an ill-fated "Spanish" dancer in a New Mexico town. (Val Lewton's horror classic was one of the first in that genre to feature Hispanic-American characters; atypically, the villain was Anglo.)

Margo (1917-1985) believed, "Although I was credited with helping introduce the rhumba, I always thought I should rely on my acting ability. I knew that people's new-found fascination with South America could only last a few years, and it was mostly politically inspired, though it was a very happy time for us." After retiring from films, she and Eddie Albert did a popular nightclub act in the '50s in such posh spots as the Waldorf Astoria, and later devoted her efforts to the arts in the Los Angeles Hispanic community with her daughter.

1940 marked the screen birth of Cuban Desi Arnaz (né Desiderio Alberto Arnaz y de Acha) in TOO MANY GIRLS, starring Lucille Ball. The film was based on a Broadway musical in which Arnaz (1917-1986) had been featured. Symbolically, the fiery young Latin was bracketed in flames while he sang the movie's big production number. Arnaz had already apprenticed under "Cugie," then led a rival band, and would continue primarily as a band leader and singer till 1951 and "I Love Lucy." As he admitted in *A Book*, after wedding Ball, "I could have stayed home and been kept by my wife."

Instead, he energetically propagated the Latin Sound until long after its height, especially—and more often in Spanish than English—via '50s television, as Ricky Ricardo. He also found time for movies. For instance, he was fourth-billed in 1941's FOUR JACKS AND A JILL, as taxi driver Michael Henley. Arnaz's white skin allowed him to essay the non-Hispanic character—with a strong Cuban accent!—as well as the fellow's look-alike, King Stephan VIII, for which part his voice was dubbed.

In 1943, Arnaz had a rare dramatic role in MGM's BATAAN, the story of a handful of men who defend a bridge so that General MacArthur can escape the Philippines. This was one of very few WWII films indicating the Hispanic presence in the American war effort. Arnaz played Felix Ramirez, a "jitterbug kid" from California who dies early on.*

*In 1982, he played the last of his now-rare movie roles in THE ESCAPE ARTIST, using the name Desiderio Arnaz. He said at the time that his son Desi, Jr. was now Desi and that it was his time for a career.

Duncan Renaldo as the Cisco Kid

Gilbert Roland and Chris-Pin Martin as Cisco Kid and Pancho

BATAAN may legitimately be accused of tokenism, but it was a start, for in 1945 came BACK TO BATAAN, this time with Anthony Quinn, as a Filipino patriot,

Capt. Andres Bonifacio, who is recruited by—who else?—John Wayne to fight the Japanese and help the Allied cause.

Two years previously, Quinn had been featured in GUADALCANAL DIARY as Soose, a Mexican-American marine private who is the sole survivor of a danger-laden patrol on Guadalcanal. The picture was a near-factual retelling of the celebrated marine invasion of August, 1942, in which the strategic island was taken after four months of fierce fighting.

1943 also yielded perhaps the first noble-Hispanic-martyr role, with Quinn playing "Mexican" in William Wellman's THE OX-BOW INCIDENT, starring Henry Fonda. As a suspected cattle rustler, Quinn and Anglo companions Dana Andrews and Francis Ford (John's brother) are sacrificed to mob rule. The film, an anti-lynching indictment, was based on a true story of 1885, in which the three hanged men were later found to have been innocent. "Mexican" tries to escape, is shot, then bravely extracts a bullet from his own leg. Though he is lynched, he dies with dignity and honor intact, reversing traditional images of the cowardly, cringing Hispanic.

In the 1946 CALIFORNIA, directed by John Farrow (Mia's father), the ever-busy Quinn essayed Don Luis Rivera y Hernandez, a dignified Spanish marquis, in a tale of early California romantically pairing Barbara Stanwyck with Ray Milland. Quinn's was "a peripheral role," and he was quoted ten years later, "In the '40s I had a lot of roles with wonderful potential, characters who might have held up a story on their own, but were always watching the Anglo-Saxon actor and actress have a courtship . . ."

Social injustice south of the border was poetically delineated in Emilio "El Indio" Fernandez's Mexican classic MARIA CANDELARIA (1943). Set in Mexico City's Floating Gardens of Xochimilco, it is the love story of Maria (Dolores Del Rio) and Lorenzo (Pedro Armendariz). It's also the story of how an Indian community shuns the virtuous title character at every turn because her late mother was a prostitute. A subplot illustrates a mestizo merchant's exploitation of the Indians.

After the villagers glimpse a nude portrait by a white painter from the city, they stone Maria to death. Too late, the mob finds out that she only posed for the head . . . "Heartbreakingly beauti-

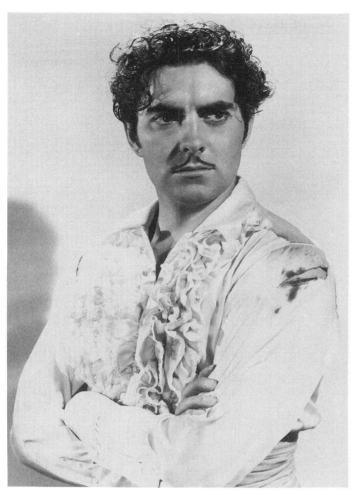

Tyrone Power in THE MARK OF ZORRO (1940)

The controversial film received scant play in the U.S., but critic Arthur Pettit found that despite "The simple dichotomy of Good Church versus Bad State, which is as irritating as it is fictitious . . . THE FUGITIVE remains the most sympathetic approach to Latin Catholicism in Hollywood's history."

Del Rio didn't return to Hollywood until 1960 (to portray Elvis Presley's mother), after the McCarthy era. During the 1950s she was barred from the U.S., for having aided anti-Franco refugees from the Spanish Civil War.

Hollywood's other top Mexican actress also departed in the early 1940s, but not temporarily. After carrying on through eight Mexican Spitfire entries, Lupe Velez's career was washed up. It had been an eventful journey from San Luis Potosi to

ful," said *Lo Nuestro* magazine, while *Look* called PORTRAIT OF MARIA (its U.S. and U.K. title) "a doomed, haunting tale of man's inhumanity to woman." Like all Fernandez's films, MARIA CANDE-LARIA brought the *indio* and mestizo to the center-stage once reserved for paler characters. When it finally got to France, MARIA won the 1946 Cannes Film Festival's grand prize.

Del Rio's first four Mexican films were helmed by Fernandez, and through the '40s and '50s, she consolidated her position as preeminent Mexican actress. Her sole "foreign" movie during this period was John Ford's 1947 THE FUGITIVE, based on Graham Greene's novel *The Power and the Glory*, set in Mexico during the anticlerical reforms of the '20s and '30s. Oddly—or not—Henry Fonda starred as a tippling Mexican priest who begets an illegitimate child. Del Rio played a self-sacrificing mother.

Tyrone Power in BLOOD AND SAND (1941)

Tyrone Power in
CAPTAIN FROM CASTILE (1947)

Lupe Velez isn't too happy to find Marion Martin in Buddy Rogers' lap in
THE MEXICAN SPITFIRE'S BABY (1941)

Lupe Velez and friends in SIX
LESSONS FROM MADAME LA
ZONGA (1940)

Lupe Velez with Leon Errol (left), Don Barclay and Luis Alberni (right in
THE MEXICAN SPITFIRE'S ELEPHANT (1942)

Lupe Velez's hijinks in LADIES' DAY (1943)

The second major trend vis-á-vis screen Hispanics in the 1940s—apart from their musicalization—was verisimilitude. For the first time, and regardless of the motives, an ongoing attempt was made to be truthful about Hispanic subjects. Now that the Latin American market was so important, its reaction to Hollywood's product was significant. Crude and derogatory pictures provoked angry demonstrations or even riots in cities like Bogota, Mexico City and Buenos Aires. One movie, ARGENTINE NIGHTS, resulted in a burned-down Argentine theatre.

Hollywood therefore opened an International Information Center to help writers, directors and producers in obviating negative and misleading portrayals before a film was made. When the Office didn't do a thorough enough job, local governments sometimes took matters into their own hands. After director John Huston shot his on-location footage for THE TREASURE OF THE SIERRA MADRE (1948), Mexico's Department of the Interior seized the film. Tampico's mayor, Fernando San Pedro, banned the Warners crew from filming in run-down areas of the city where "drunks, ragged, dirty beggars, and others astride gaunt burros were depicted by the actors." Thus, the film's border-

Beverly Hills, where Lupe dwelled in a "fake hacienda on Rodeo Drive." But where to go from there? Her last turn as the choleric Carmelita (whose surname sometimes changed unaccountably) was in THE MEXICAN SPITFIRE'S BLESSED EVENT (1943).

Ironically, when Velez became pregnant in real life, she declined to have an abortion, but then the father declined to marry her, and so, at a beauteous 36 (the same age as Marilyn Monroe), she snuffed out her life with a pill overdose.

Lupe Velez committed suicide in 1944 after her affair with French actor Harald Ramond (sic)

SINTOWN (1942) featured Leo Carrillo and Constance Bennett

town sequences were "considerably cleaned up to satisfy the Mexican authorities."

Another factor in the growing authenticity of Hispanic-themed films was the emergence after WWII of co-productions between U.S. and Latin American studios. Such movies were often shot on location with Hispanic crews and sometimes Hispanic actors. THE FUGITIVE was one such picture, and though it flopped in America, it did well south of the border. In fact, even after the war the Pan-American market for Hollywood's output was considerable; by 1949, 20 Latin Western Hemisphere nations accounted for nearly one-fifth of the foreign market for American films. In other words, less than 10 percent of the world's population supplied about 20 percent of foreign film royalties.

Betty Grable, the top box office star of the '40s, male or female, asserted in *Look* magazine, "Hollywood put me on the map, but South America also helped . . . I might not be where I am today without those swell Latin musicals!" Grable's big break occurred when an ailing Alice Faye had to forego DOWN ARGENTINE WAY (1940). Grable stepped in, and the film was a smash hit. In Argentina and else-

MEXICANA (1945) starred Tito Guizar and Leo Carrillo

Singer Tito Guizar and Virginia Bruce in BRAZIL (1944)

where too, for Fox had been persuaded by the Motion Picture Section of the Office of the Coordinator of Inter-American Affairs to spend an additional $40,000 to reshoot scenes from the picture which falsely depicted local customs.

In RKO's 1941 THEY MET IN ARGENTINA, starring Irish Maureen O'Hara as a native, an effort was made to compare life in Argentina with American life. For the sake of wartime inter-American unity, American audiences were shown "that North and South America were quite similar." Re Allen Woll, in his essay "The Latin Image in American Film":

> Co-star Buddy Ebsen is surprised to find everyone from secretaries to ranch hands is able to speak English with only the slightest trace of accent . . . that Argentine immigration patterns in the 19th century paralleled those of the United States . . . that the gauchos of THEY MET IN ARGENTINA sing the same song that the North American hero sang as a youth on his Texas ranch.

During the war, the on-screen lives of Hispanic people tended to be extravagant, even fantastic. Negativism was drastically reduced, but Holly-

THE GAY RANCHERO (1947) billed Roy Rogers (here with Jan Frazee and Andy Devine) and even Trigger over Tito Guizar

wood waited until after the war—when the morale-boosting music suddenly seemed to stop—to focus on average Hispanic people living *within* the U.S. border.

"The war changed everything," said Thomas Gomez, né Sabino Tomas Gomez (1905-1971). The stout actor, who spoke flawless English, entered movies in his thirties, via SHERLOCK HOLMES AND THE VOICE OF TERROR (1942). "After the war, I still did stock Latin roles, but fewer of them. After the war, I was treated with more respect, and people stopped using words like 'Spic,' at least openly . . . Hollywood was more careful about us, on the screen and off. That lasted until about the 1960s."

In 1961's SUMMER AND SMOKE, adapted from the play by Tennessee Williams, Gomez as Rita Moreno's father did a greaser role which infuriated many Hispanic-Americans and led to demonstrations in several cities. He stayed away from the screen until 1968. Gomez's other films include ARABIAN NIGHTS and DEAD MAN'S EYES with Acquanetta, CAPTAIN FROM CASTILE (1947) with Cesar Romero, KEY LARGO (1948), I MARRIED A COMMUNIST (1949) and MACAO (1952).

The little-seen Paramount film A MEDAL FOR BENNY (1945) was a turning point in the depiction of Hispanics. No extravaganza, it derived from a

Frank Sinatra and a "greaser" (note the exaggerated nose!) in THE KISSING BANDIT (1948)

Donna Reed and Connie Gilchrist go Hispanic in APACHE TRAIL (1942)

Rita Hayworth and Steven Geray (as Uncle Pio) in GILDA (1946)

John Steinbeck story, and was possibly the first picture where the Anglos were the bad guys and the Hispanics the good guys. A native of the fictitious town of Pantera, California, Benny, who is never seen, is posthumously awarded a Congressional Medal of Honor for "killing 100 Japs." All at once, the townspeople who had ignored Benny and the other Hispanic citizens have a change of heart.

Or, rather, a change of pocketbook. The Anglo town fathers hope that the awarding ceremony and its well-publicized celebration will attract tourists, investors and an economic boom. Benny's father

Charlie (J. Carrol Naish) is granted a bank loan he had repeatedly requested but been refused. Charlie is temporarily put up in a local mansion, pending the ceremony, but departs when he realizes the hypocrisy of the situation. The Chamber of Commerce pleads in vain, "You get the glory and we get the gravy."

The mayor and a five-star general search for Charlie in the barrio. "You can't go there," states the former. "It's just a lot of shacks." The latter replies, "Some mighty fine Americans have come out of shacks."

Rita Hayworth, 1940s love goddess

(*Here and on facing page*) Anthony Quinn spent much of the '40s playing Native Americans (comic and serious) and Orientals.

So Charlie receives his son's medal on his own doorstep. He tells the radio audience that "Benny's house doesn't matter, because the country must depend on all kinds of people." The message is clear, that Hispanic-Americans are here to stay. In the film's opening, a title card describes them as "a simple, friendly people who were the original settlers of California." For once, in the words of one reviewer, "The Chicanos here display the admirable traits which their Anglo brethren seem to lack." They also, for a change, are shown having personal lives and relationships; one Joe Morales (Arturo de Cordova) has a love life, wooing and even winning Dorothy Lamour, unlike male Hispanics of previous decades.

Post-WWII, there was another welcome change in Hollywood portraits of Hispanics. More and more, they were in the forefront, where once they'd been relegated to a story's background—as local color. And if Hispanic characters were still frequently represented by Anglo actors, at least those characters were more central, and decreasingly villainous or stereotypical. Besides, in the case of films like THE FUGITIVE, it could be argued that without a box office star like Henry Fonda in the lead, the

picture would have gotten even poorer distribution, if made at all.

As in A MEDAL FOR BENNY, the tendency was toward better-rounded Hispanic characters. Increasingly, they were assigned a specific national heritage—usually Mexican—rather than the vague label of "Spanish" or the cardboard "mixed." (An exception to this trend was "half-breed" Pearl Chavez [Jennifer Jones], the swarthy, promiscuous villainess of unspecified background—is she part-Native American?—in David O. Selznick's 1946 Western epic DUEL IN THE SUN.)

The Old Southwest and Early California—with their "pure-blooded" because Castilian characters—fell out of vogue after the war, with a few exceptions. As previously noted, Zorro was a recurring phenomenon, incarnated in 1940 by Tyrone Power, crossing swords with his dictatorial nemesis Captain Juan Ramon (Basil Rathbone, whose dark, menacing looks often found him as villains and/or Latins.) THE MARK OF ZORRO, directed by Rouben Mamoulian, utilized lavish production values to offset the fact that Power made a much less athletic Zorro than Fairbanks had.

Power also played Latin in Mamoulian's 1941

Actress-dancer Margo and Dennis O'Keefe in THE LEOPARD MAN (1943)

THE LEOPARD MAN was a rare horror film with a Hispanic setting

96

Joseph Cotten and "half-breed" Pearl Chavez (Jennifer Jones) in DUEL IN THE SUN (1946)

remake of Blasco Ibañez's BLOOD AND SAND (a 1922 Valentino vehicle). Its other Spaniards were Rita Hayworth (as the fiery redheaded mistress), Linda Darnell (as the ideal brunette wife), Russian Alla Nazimova, John Carradine and Laird Cregar. The only Hispanic playing a major character was Anthony Quinn; and, as a specialty dancer, Elena Verdugo of later MARCUS WELBY, M.D. television fame.

Due to stricter censorship, certain 1922 scenes with Nita Naldi as Doña Sol couldn't be recreated with Rita Hayworth. However, the erotic tension of a dance performed by Hayworth and Quinn in a smoke-filled Spanish *boîte* was not so easily omitted. Critic Charles Greenberg wrote, "Above all, the scenes in the *corrida*, passionately directed and filled with thousands of Mexican extras, are perhaps the most thrilling of their kind ever filmed, with their justly famous shot of the purple contents of a burst wineskin spilling on a white napkin to signal the bull's offscreen death." Most critics were divided as to whether Valentino or Power made the better Latin Lover.

Power was Spanish again in 1947's CAPTAIN

Gloria De Haven and Carlos Ramirez in TWO GIRLS AND A SAILOR (1944)

Darryl Hickman, Esther Fernandez and Alan Ladd in TWO YEARS BEFORE THE MAST (1946)

Martha Stewart, Olga San Juan and Patricia Dane in ARE YOU WITH IT? (1948)

98

José Iturbi, Jane Powell, Jeanette MacDonald along with Ann E. Todd (left) and Mary Elinor Donahue (right, later of FATHER KNOWS BEST) in THREE DARING DAUGHTERS (1948)

FROM CASTILE (Antonio Moreno played his father). Maybe because of his handsome coloring, or his aptness for such roles, certain Latin American publications, including *Lo Nuestro*, erroneously—or wishfully—attributed to him "Latin blood." This time, Ty was a Spanish nobleman escaping the Inquisition by sailing to the New World with Cortez (Cesar Romero). *Lo Nuestro* observed, "In the naîve Hollywood retelling, Cortez is *not* a blood-thirsty, greedy misanthrope, and the Aztecs are almost relieved to be conquered by the white Spaniards!"

Hollywood continued to misrepresent or misunderstand Mexico's ethnic complexities—in rigid Colonial pecking order: Spanish, creole, mestizo and Indian. Other American nations were more easily portrayed: Costa Rica, for example, whose people are predominantly of European descent. Cesar Romero was a convincing Costa Rican in the florid CARNIVAL IN COSTA RICA. But Vera-Ellen, as American as apple pie, was less believable as a half-Costa Rican, the daughter of Yankee Anne Revere, who married a Costa Rican and found her way to San Jose.

The plot, sandwiched between native scenery, Vera-Ellen's dances and Dick Haymes' songs, concerns arranged marriage. Local customs go awry when Vera-Ellen falls for a visiting Gringo and Romero for a visiting Gringa (Celeste Holm). The three traditionalist parents are up in arms, but the wise American mom scores points for modernism when she approves and enables her daughter's marriage to the man she favors over Romero. The paterfamilias' ego is assuaged when Revere informs him that he cannot reject his future son-in-law because "I gave him your consent . . ."

This screen disparity, the alleged sexual superior-

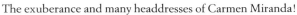
The exuberance and many headdresses of Carmen Miranda!

ity of the North American male, refused to disappear in the 1940s. Back in the '30s, in FLYING DOWN TO RIO, Dolores had been easily pried from the arms of her Brazilian fiancé by a Yankee bandleader. In the 1941 THEY MET IN ARGENTINA, local Maureen O'Hara is readily stolen by James Ellison from her boyfriend Alberto Vila. The same thing transpires in the RKO films TOO MANY GIRLS (1940) and PAN-AMERICANA (1945).

But back to Cesar. In 1940 and '41, Romero starred in six Cisco Kid adventures, i.e., LUCKY CISCO KID, VIVA CISCO KID! and THE GAY CABALLERO . . . After Romero, the series disappeared, then in 1945 Monogram took it over from Fox. Duncan Renaldo did 12 episodes (including later ones for United Artists) between 1945 and '50, and Gilbert Roland did six during 1946-7. But it was Renaldo (1904-1980) who became most closely

John Payne, Carmen Miranda and Cesar Romero in SPRINGTIME IN THE ROCKIES (1942)

Perry Como, Carmen Miranda, Martha Stewart and Dennis O'Keefe in DOLL FACE (1945)

Denis (sic) Quilley (in PRIVATES ON PARADE, 1984), one of countless Carmen Miranda impersonators over the years

associated with the role, via 156 half-hour TV shows (the syndicated serial would go on to earn the largest receipts of its time).

Modeled after O. Henry's 1907 short story "The Caballero's Way," the Kid roamed the Southwest in the decades following the American conquest. "The Cisco Kid had killed six men in more or less fair scrimmage, had murdered twice as many, mostly Mexicans, and had winged a large number whom he modestly forebore to count." So began the story, but not the series, in which the Kid was distinctly non-violent. He was an action hero, but not *too* active, and a romantic figure, but not *too* much so.

Raoul Walsh directed the 1929 IN OLD ARIZONA, and lost one eye during its filming. He believed the secret of the ambiguous (but "pure-blooded") hero's success was that "He threatened nobody. He did good deeds, didn't outstay his welcome, had a sense of humor, and if at times he flirted with white women, marriage was out of the question." He was

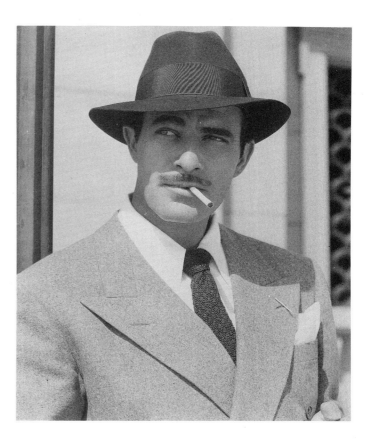

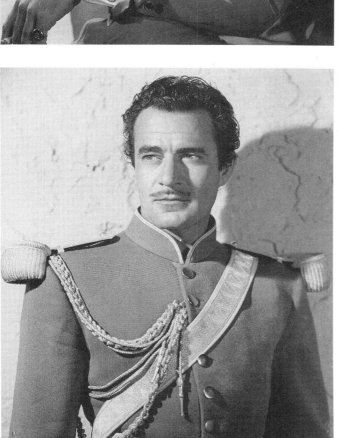

Gilbert Roland in PIRATES OF MONTEREY (1947)

also idolized by his contrastingly inept, semi-greaser sidekick Pancho, who provided ostensible comic relief. Next to the Lone Ranger and Tonto, the Latino cowboy-hero and Pancho were "the most fabulous and fantastic pair of Good Guys on the range," invariably ending each adventure with the exchange "Oh, Pancho! Oh, Ceesco! Oh, ho, ho!"

In his book *They Went Thataway*, James Horwitz explained why Fox dropped the Cisco Kid. ". . . The role was taken over by Cesar Romero, with Chris-Pin Martin as Pancho. Romero was no cowboy, but one of those Brill-creamed Latin Lover types, and played the Kid as a smarmy dandy and fop, while Martin's Pancho was a gutbucket slob. Latin American sensibilities were offended by this unlikely duo. An international incident nearly occurred. Diplomatic cables flew back and forth between Latin America and the State Department. The Cisco Kid, as portrayed by Romero, was, so to speak, queering America's south-of-the-border for-

Gilbert Roland and Errol Flynn in THE SEA HAWK (1940)

Singer-actress Lina Romay

eign policy. Darryl Zanuck at Fox was more or less ordered by Washington to change Cisco's style or stop making the pictures. He decided to drop the series altogether."

The replacement of the "mincing Romero" with a "lecherous Roland" proved unpopular in the U.S. *and* abroad; Romero had been a very popular Kid in the U.S. Horwitz described the new Cisco as "a typical Rolandesque cigarillo-smoking, hot-sweat-of-passion, lusty, mucho macho caballero. The films bombed out."

It was Renaldo who hit the right note of inoffensive asexuality and non-violence, and became *the* Cisco Kid. But it was a long, torturous road to fame. Renaldo's first big role was in the 1929 THE BRIDGE OF SAN LUIS REY. He then spent two years in Africa making TRADER HORN, but on January 17, 1931, just before TRADER HORN's gala premiere at Grauman's Chinese Theatre in Hollywood, he was arrested and charged with being an illegal immigrant and making false statements about his place of birth in order to obtain a passport.

Lina Romay with Mickey Rooney in LOVE LAUGHS AT ANDY HARDY (1945)

The next six years saw Renaldo indicted by a Grand Jury, taken to court for trial, served with several contempt of court citations, convicted of perjury and making false statements, sentenced to two years in a federal jail—he served 18 months on McNeil Island—and then chased out of the U.S. by Immigration authorities who wanted to deport him. Renaldo had to live on a friend's boat out beyond the three-mile limit, for the U.S. government wouldn't let him land. Finally, in 1936, the actor who'd been on the verge of stardom at the beginning of the decade was granted an unconditional Presidential pardon by FDR. But his involvement with the law, and his jail term, made it difficult for him to find employment, and he had to wait until 1945 to become the Cisco Kid.

As a Kid who pleased domestic and foreign audiences alike, Renaldo told the author, "The Cisco Kid never killed anyone. We tricked the bandits into killing each other off . . . After the trouble Fox had with the series, we didn't want any complaints. So I went to Mexico for three weeks at the Inter-American Relations Committee, and we devised a format acceptable to Latin governments. I asked,

Lina Romay and Xavier Cugat in TWO GIRLS AND A SAILOR (1944)

105

Lina Romay and Xavier Cugat in BATHING BEAUTY (1944)

'Why don't we pattern the Cisco Kid after Don Quixote, and Pancho after Sancho Panza?'

"They sprang for the idea like *that*, and I designed the costume myself. I made it connect somehow with each of the Latin countries. For instance, the belts were Argentine and Ecuadorian. The hat was Mexican . . . By the time I got done with it, it was a representative amalgamation of Latin America!"

Leo Carrillo's tenure as Pancho helped to some extent to neutralize his former image as a greaser *par* non-*excellence*. Renaldo revealed, "The Mexican government was not the only one which warned Leo that he might become *persona non grata* in their country if he didn't downplay the pernicious greaser-type." As Pancho, he was still a buffoon, but no longer pernicious.

In the 1970s, there was talk about the Cisco Kid returning to the screen. But after the dismal failure of the costly LONE RANGER remake, any such plans were shelved. In 1979, there was THE FRISCO KID, a parody with Gene Wilder as a way-out-West Polish rabbi. And the rock group *War* immortalized the Kid and his sidekick in a hit song: "The Cisco Kid was a friend o' mine . . ."

Thus, the screen Hispanic was becoming more familiar, less a threat, particularly via social problem and musical films, e.g., the congenial Desi Arnaz in CUBAN PETE (1946). Hispanics were also becoming more familiar in real life, for WWII accelerated the demand for agricultural labor, met by a new flow of immigrants into the Southwest's barrios and *colonias*. With the postwar economic boom, immigration continued, from Mexico, Central and South America, and the Caribbean.

But the sometimes invisible minority which *Life* called "the minority nobody knows" was still ill-

Lina Romay and Xavier Cugat in WEEKEND AT THE WALDORF (1945)

Orson Welles and Dolores Del Rio at CITIZEN KANE's premiere (1941)

Dolores Del Rio and Joseph Cotten in JOURNEY INTO FEAR

Dolores Del Rio in Orson Welles' JOURNEY INTO FEAR (1942)

served in several movies, still serving as bandits, scapegoats or pawns. At least the Mexican outlaw enacted by Alfonso Bedoya in 1948's THE TREASURE OF THE SIERRA MADRE managed to steal several scenes from Humphrey Bogart. According to Arthur Pettit, "Elevated to an existential hero who faces death with honor, Bedoya shows qualities of courage, wit and pride foreign to the stock Hollywood bandido."

In Howard Hawks' 1948 RED RIVER, when two Mexicans question John Wayne's right to take over the entire Rio Grande watershed as his private cattle preserve, they are routinely dispatched by quickdraw Wayne. One critic wrote of a Hispanic villain in another film, "Nor has the target become any handier with his fists over the decades." In any number of major or minor Westerns of the time, one or two Anglo heroes are able to triumph over a superior number of clumsy, barroom-brawling Hispanics.

1949's BORDER INCIDENT presented two of the "scurviest, low-downed-est *hombres* ever" to reach the screen, said *Time*. But it was "okay," because Alfonso Bedoya and Arnold Moss are in the pay of a snake-eyed American racketeer, played by Howard da Silva.

Even though the leading Latin star of the 1940s

Dolores Del Rio and Pedro Armendariz in MARIA CANDELARIA (1943)

Dolores Del Rio in LA OTRA (The Other Woman, 1946)

Dolores Del Rio in LAS ABANDONADAS (Abandoned Women, 1944)

was a female, three-dimensional film characterizations of Latinas lagged well behind those of men. This was, and continues to be, due to the sexism which overlaps the standard racism and xenophobia. The celluloid Latina was either "a looney-Latin figure of fun" (as *Photoplay* called Carmen Miranda) or a dangerous doyenne of the bedroom. *Lo Nuestro* was galled by "the deliberate fact that the worst of these implied nymphomaniacs ascribed to us are played by untalented foreigners!"

There was, for example, the "half-breed" Rio, embodied by Jane Russell in Howard Hughes' notorious THE OUTLAW (1943). Officially about Billy the Kid, the picture garnered massive publicity concerning Russell's shocking cleavage. In 1946, Linda Darnell shed her mantilla from BLOOD AND SAND and her good-gal image to play the strumpet Chihuahua in John Ford's MY DARLING CLEMENTINE (the title character is a chaste Bostonian miss). After being passed from Victor Mature to Henry Fonda, Chihuahua engages in an affair with young John Ireland. As per the movie Code, she then must die for her "sins."

Arturo De Cordova and Ann Dvorak in MASQUERADE IN MEXICO (1945)

Dolores Del Rio in HISTORIA DE UNA MALA MUJER (Lady Windermere's Fan, 1948)

Arturo De Cordova and Betty Hutton in INCENDIARY BLONDE (1945)

Dolores Del Rio and Henry Fonda in THE FUGITIVE (1947)
(*On facing page*)

Maria Montez, siren supreme

112

Carmen Miranda never had any on-screen sins. She just had and created fun, and was sometimes made fun of. Neé Maria do Carmo Miranda da Cunha, she made her Brazilian screen debut in 1933. For five years, she was a favorite of Portuguese-language movie audiences—only. In 1934, Ramon Novarro went to Rio to promote his cousin Dolores' FLYING DOWN TO RIO (which he wasn't in), and after watching Carmen perform in a nightclub, encouraged her to go to Hollywood. Eventually she did, in a roundabout way, for she was discovered by a Fox talent scout while appearing on Broadway in the 1939 musical THE STREETS OF PARIS.

Fox cautiously introduced the bizarre *Brasileira* in Betty Grable's DOWN ARGENTINE WAY (1940)— Carmen had no spoken dialogue. But in 1941 she blossomed like a gaudy orchid in the Alice Faye musicals THAT NIGHT IN RIO and WEEKEND IN HAVANA. She hit her peak in the 1942 SPRINGTIME IN THE ROCKIES (with Grable, Romero and John Payne) and in Busby Berkeley's 1943 camp spectacular THE GANG'S ALL HERE (with Faye and John Payne, and Carmen in a towering banana head-

Maria Montez, Turhan Bey and servant girl in ALI BABA AND THE FORTY THIEVES (1943)

Jon Hall, Maria Montez, Sidney Toler and Sabu in WHITE SAVAGE (1943)

dress). By 1944, she was down to guest star musical turns in FOUR JILLS IN A JEEP, GREENWICH VILLAGE and SOMETHING FOR THE BOYS. "Hollywood," she learned, "is just like a rolley-coaster!"

COPACABANA in 1947 was her last starring role. The next year, she parodied her now-renowned "looney-Latin" in A DATE WITH JUDY, starring Jane Powell and Elizabeth Taylor. Not coincidentally,

Miranda's rise and fall paralleled that of the Good Neighbor Policy.

The 1940s saw the rise of other Latin stars who, if they didn't flash as quickly or brightly as Miranda, had longer careers. Not so the gorgeous Dominican Republic-born Maria Montez (1918-1951). Neé Maria Africa Antonia Gracia Vidal de Santo Silas, she debuted in 1940 and made her last films in

(*Here, and on facing page*) Maria Montez in her most famous film, COBRA WOMAN (1944)

Maria Montex with Lon Chaney, Jr., and Lois Colier in COBRA WOMAN

1950. Montez possessed a flaming beauty and sexuality akin to Lupe Velez's, but unlike Velez didn't have to camouflage or distort them in antic comedies.

Montez was fortunate in having Universal build lavish Technicolor "Easterns" around her. They often co-starred Jon Hall and Turhan Bey or Sabu, and over the years several have become cult classics, like ARABIAN NIGHTS (1942), COBRA WOMAN (1944), SUDAN (1945), TANGIER (1946), PIRATES OF MONTEREY (1947) with Gilbert Roland, and, with husband Jean-Pierre Aumont SIREN OF ATLANTIS (1948).

Unusually for a Latin, Montez usually played authority figures. She always dominated the nefarious proceedings, and functioned as a sex symbol in diverse nationalities. Off screen as well, she took her career very seriously. She told *Screenland* magazine in 1944 how she'd engineered her Hollywood rise: "I made it a point to be seen wherever the producers went—Ciro's, Mocambo, . . . I spent hours designing gowns and hats that would obligate everyone to look at me when I entered. I went to Max Factor's, and consulted with Frederick, the best hair stylist for unusual coiffures.

Maria Montez and George Zucco in SUDAN (1945)

Maria Montez in SIREN OF ATLANTIS (1948)

Pre-Hollywood Ricardo Montalban in Mexico (with Isabela Corona)

"My name was unknown, and this was my method of attracting attention to me, for the sake of publicity and for the sake of acquiring the interest of producers."

Though Montez's first and final films cast her as peripheral girlfriends, she strove to avoid the disposable-Latina syndrome. "For me, being a movie star means being the most important character in a movie . . . and not being constrained by one's real-life background. I am proud of who I am, I play proud characters, and I cannot play women who are pushed or laughed at." It would be interesting to speculate what a middle-aged Montez's career might have been like, and whether, like Dolores Del Rio, she would have grown as a dramatic actress.

Tragically, she died at 33—drowned in her scalding bath, after a possible heart attack.

While Montez briefly captured Hollywood's fancy, the proud and beautiful Maria Felix (born Maria de los Angeles Felix Guereña in 1915) eventually conquered Mexican cinema. Her screen bow was the 1942 EL PEÑON DE LAS ÁNIMAS (*The Rock of Souls*). Felix's only competition as queen of Mexi-

Ricardo Montalban and Esther Williams in ON AN ISLAND WITH YOU (1948)

117

Rita Hayworth in THE LOVES OF CARMEN (1948)

Rita Hayworth

can film was Del Rio, who later abdicated (she made only five Mexican pictures between 1960 and 1978).

1942 witnessed the movie debuts in Argentina and Mexico of Fernando Lamas and Ricardo Montalban, respectively. Both would move to Hollywood and become, in the '50s and '60s, the top Hispanic actors in American film, with subsequent careers in television. Another '50s star, Katy Jurado, debuted in Mexico in 1943. And in 1944, Spain's stunning, sultry Sara Montiel made her screen bow. Known in Latin America as Sarita Montiel (born 1928), she had a go at Hollywood, and in 1954 starred with Gary Cooper and Burt Lancaster in VERA CRUZ.

"They cast me as a Mexican, then gave me fewer and fewer lines. By the end of my stay in Holly-

Anthony Quinn in IRISH EYES ARE SMILING (1944)

The Three Mesquiteers: Tom Tyler, Jimmie Dodd and Bob Steele

Maria Montez

Brazilian bombshell Carmen Miranda

Jane Russell as "Rio" in THE OUTLAW (1943)

Alice Faye and Carmen Miranda in WEEKEND IN HAVANA (1941)

wood, I no longer felt like an actress." Montiel worked in Mexican cinema, through which she became a superstar all over Latin America, then returned to Spain, where she is an ageless institution.

Asked in the 1970s if she would give Hollywood another try, she responded, "Oh, no! They do not understand their own women, let alone foreign ones . . ."

Alfonso Bedoya and Humphrey Bogart in THE TREASURE OF THE SIERRA MADRE (1948)

120

Walter Huston, Humphrey Bogart, Tim Holt and unidentified Mexicans in THE
TREASURE OF THE SIERRA MADRE

Cantinflas with Marlene Dietrich and Red Skelton in AROUND THE WORLD IN 80
DAYS

4. THE FIFTIES:
Myths & Machismo

"Hollywood perpetuates two myths about the Latin male. One, that he is a tyrant. In fact, he may have more freedom to roam, but the Latin woman rules the home. And two, he is a better lover. He is not a better lover—he just spends less time conversing . . ."
—Fernando Lamas in *Silver Screen*, 1975

Like the economically ravaged 1930s, the booming 1950s were a time of looking inward, even though Hollywood movies began shooting overseas in big numbers, for the first time. And the Eisenhower years were politically very conservative, with "un-American" a byword for alleged subversion. Yet during this time, the movie Code was effectively challenged, minority civil rights were brought up, and Hispanics became more politically aware than ever. Screen treatments of Hispanics included some of the best up until that time.

And yet . . . By 1950, Carmen Miranda had gone from amusing ex-fad in the late '40s to a show biz joke. That year, she appeared in NANCY GOES TO RIO, starring Jane Powell. After two difficult years without a film—for Carmen was a workaholic and a born worrier, her carefree image notwithstand-

ing—she made one last picture in 1953, SCARED STIFF, a Dean Martin and Jerry Lewis remake of Bob Hope's 1940 THE GHOST BREAKERS. In it, Lewis impersonated the lady with the platform wedgies and the edible headdresses.

Before, and since, she had become one of the most imitated of movie stars. Other Carmen copies include Mickey Rooney in BABES ON BROADWAY (1941), Bob Hope in THE ROAD TO RIO (1947), Carol Burnett in CHU CHU AND THE PHILLY FLASH (1981) and NBC "Today Show" weatherman Willard Scott in 1984. By the time of her death at 46 in 1955, Carmen Miranda had become a legend, giving her all to her music and roles. Not surprisingly, she died of an occlusion of the coronaries—her heart had been worn out.

The Latina's celluloid heyday was over. Holly-

Latin lover Richard "Chito" Martin, Tim Holt's sidekick

wood would never again, to date, experience Hispanic leading ladies of the magnitude of Dolores Del Rio, Lupe Velez, Carmen Miranda and Maria Montez. Ethnic was *out*, until the 1970s, and "whitebread" was in. It was also the macho's turn to shine, as the strong female stars who rose before the war were shunted to one side. The likes of Davis, Hepburn, Crawford and Stanwyck were replaced with a passel of pliable blondes: Marilyn, Debbie, Doris, Jane Powell, Judy Holliday, June Allyson and so on.

After eight years of Mexican films, Katy Jurado (born Maria Jurado Garcia in 1927) was brought to Hollywood in 1951 for—what else?—THE BULLFIGHTER AND THE LADY. A publicity handout described her as "A dark-haired Mexican actress with pouting lips and flashing eyes. With those looks, Katy really couldn't have come from anywhere else!" *Ole!*

She hit her Hollywood peak in 1952 as Helen Ramirez in Fred Zinneman's Gary Cooper classic (and anti-McCarthy Western) HIGH NOON. Though Helen, like CLEMENTINE's Chihuahua, is a rejected lover, her guts, compassion and dignity are atypical of screen Latinas. Helen is also wealthy, the owner of a store and saloon. Still, she is an outcast, not only for her heritage, but because she is unmarried, lives well and flaunts the community's mores. Neither flighty nor fickle, she has nonetheless enjoyed affairs with both the film's villain and hero.

The latter, Will Kane (Cooper), has been hired by the townfolk to restore law and order. Helen backs the good man against the bad, and berates the townspeople for not standing behind Kane, whose mouthpiece and symbolic conscience she becomes. If she were still Kane's woman, she says, she would get a gun and fight with him—unlike Kane's imported blonde bride (Grace Kelly) from back East, for whom he threw over his mistress Helen (whom he never considers as marriage material).

Critic Wyatt Cooper felt, "Jurado defines and acts on the key moral position in HIGH NOON. An outsider, she recognizes the importance of Kane's lone stand against the threatening bully and the fearful, hypocritical townfolk. It is Jurado who foresees that 'When he dies, this town dies too.'"

There was a small outcry when Jurado didn't receive even an Oscar nomination for HIGH NOON.

Three caballeros: co-stars Antonio Moreno, Gilbert Roland and Ramon Novarro in CRISIS (1950)

It was lost in the vortex of the film's publicity, which mostly had to do with Cooper's comeback and his second Oscar, newcomer Kelly (who two years later won a Best Actress Oscar) and the film's politics—John Wayne called it "subversive."

Jurado's career didn't yield another Helen Ramirez. Instead she married Ernest Borgnine, providing Hollywood with one of its more fiery unions. The material offered her was typically inferior to her talent, and she didn't return on a long-term basis to the Mexican cinema which might have afforded her better parts. Her best post-HIGH NOON picture was the Mexican CHILDREN OF SANCHEZ (1978), now considered a minor (and little seen in the U.S.) masterpiece, co-starring Anthony Quinn and—in her last role—Dolores Del Rio. SANCHEZ was ahead of its time, as was producer Norman Lear's mid-1980s Hispanic TV sitcom, *aka Pablo*, in which Jurado played comic Paul Rodriguez's mother.

Not long after HIGH NOON, Jurado gained weight, further reducing her roles. For instance, in

ONE-EYED JACKS (1961), directed by Marlon Brando, Pina Pellicer was the romantic lead.

1950 introduced a Puerto Rican actress destined to play a wider range of parts, to win an Oscar, Emmy and Tony, and enjoy a lengthy career. Rita Moreno (neé Rosita Alverio in 1931) had two advantages over Jurado—accentless English and ongoing good looks. At first (after being "introduced" as Rosita Moreno in the vintage 1950 "chicks-in-prison" movie SO YOUNG, SO BAD and then skipping to Mario Lanza's THE TOAST OF NEW ORLEANS) she got negligible roles in diverse films like THE FABULOUS SEÑORITA, SINGIN' IN THE RAIN and MA AND PA KETTLE ON VACATION, all in 1952.

Then she graduated to what she termed "the Yonkee Peeg school of acting," portraying fierce, tempestuous Latinas, Native Americans and "half-breeds" in films starring Gary Cooper, Tyrone Power, etc. As British *Photoplay* put it, Jurado and Moreno were seldom "allowed to do much more than toss their curls, wear off-the-shoulder peasant blouses and smoulder."

But Moreno's talent and international beauty earned her meaty multi-racial roles, and in 1956 she had a great impact as the Burmese Princess Tuptim in THE KING AND I. Interestingly, despite the diversity of her roles, especially post-1950s, Moreno's two best known screen characterizations are Puerto Rican. The first, in WEST SIDE STORY (1961), made Rita Moreno the first Hispanic actress to win the Academy Award.

Meantime, the careers of Hispanic Hollywood's old-timers were winding down, usually in Westerns. Ramon Novarro made only two films in the '50s (THE OUTRIDERS and CRISIS, both 1950), while Antonio Moreno was seen in DALLAS, CRISIS, SADDLE TRAMP (all 1950) and 1954's THE CREATURE FROM THE BLACK LAGOON, among others. He tried to launch a film career in Cuba, but then Castro took over. Like Novarro with George Cukor, Moreno did finish his career in the hands of a prestige director, John Ford.

He lamented, "What we lost was glamour. In the old days, you thought of a Latin actor, you thought of glamour . . . We had looks, breeding, status. On the other hand, nowadays the whole world has lost its glamour."

The younger Gilbert Roland appeared in 1950's

THE FURIES (as Barbara Stanwyck's clandestine lover, and as a Latin, not considered marriageable), 1951's THE BULLFIGHTER AND THE LADY and 1952's THE BAD AND THE BEAUTIFUL, before playing French in THE FRENCH LINE (1954), courting a Jane Russell who'd become too big a star to play "half-breeds."

José Ferrer (né José Vicente Ferrer Otero y Cintron in 1909) made cinematic history when he became the first Hispanic actor to win an Oscar. He won Best Actor as CYRANO DE BERGERAC (1950), but returned shortly to supporting roles. Ferrer isn't generally identified as Hispanic, however; one reviewer theorized, "Maybe because his surname doesn't end in a vowel."

The accentless Ferrer has seldom played Latinos, and if anything, had his greatest successes as Frenchmen, The Dauphin in his debut JOAN OF ARC (1948), CYRANO, and Toulouse-Lautrec in MOULIN ROUGE (1952, for which he was again Oscar-nominated).

José Ferrer and Mel Ferrer have often been mistaken for each other, although no relation. The former is Puerto Rican, the latter (born 1917) is of Cuban origin. A stage director in the late Forties, Mel began his film career in 1949 but gained prominence in the '50s as the husband of Audrey Hepburn, with whom he co-starred on Broadway in ONDINE, on TV in MAYERLING, and on the screen in WAR AND PEACE (1956) and whom he directed in GREEN MANSIONS (1959), set in the Venezuelan jungle. By the 1960s (and divorce from Hepburn), Ferrer was starring in international—that is, non-Hollywood—movies, including the 1964 EL GRECO. In the early 1980s he gained wider exposure as Jane Wyman's lawyer in TV's "Falcon Crest."

After a half-decade of Mexican pictures, Ricardo Montalban (born 1920) spent seven years at MGM as a smooth-but-jealous Latin Lover. He often partnered swimming star Esther Williams, the studio's biggest moneymaker, or was seen dancing with Cyd Charisse in "specialty numbers," yet due to an accent, was always cast as Latins and other nationalities, including Japanese in SAYONARA (1957). His movies were light entertainment, i.e., THE KISSING BANDIT (1948), NEPTUNE'S DAUGHTER (1949),

(*Here, and on facing page*) Mexican superstar Maria Félix refused to work in Hollywood when they wouldn't meet her conditions

GIANT (1956), with Rock Hudson and Elizabeth Taylor had a Hispanic sub-theme

GARDEN OF EVIL (1954), with Gary Cooper and Susan Hayward employed Mexican locations—only

Fernando Lamas and Lana Turner in THE MERRY WIDOW (1952)

Lorenzo Lamas was born while Fernando was directing Jane Wyman for TV; Lorenzo and Wyman later co-starred in TV's FALCON CREST

LATIN LOVERS, AND SOMBRERO (both 1953). In the atypical (unfortunately non-hit) 1950 film MYSTERY STREET, he got to play a Hispanic police officer on Cape Cod.

In 1950 and '52 Montalban starred in two Hispanic social problem films, RIGHT CROSS and MY MAN AND I. Both followed a tinseltown formula, but it had been 15 years since BORDERTOWN, and Hispanic-Americans' problems had been mostly ignored on screen. The first of these presents Montalban as boxer Johnny Monterez, who is bitter and anti-social, believing Anglo society only tolerates him because he's a champ. Incredibly, the real problem is diagnosed as Johnny's paranoia—the problem is *his*, not society's. He arrives at this conclusion via his manager's daughter, perky June Allyson.

The two fall in love, and Allyson persuades Johnny that Americans really do like him for himself! If the film's conclusion—and its slighting of the very real discrimination facing Hispanics—seems reprehensible, at least it exhibits courage in pairing Montalban and Allyson. In 1950, the coupling of a blonde icon and even a "white Mexican" was somewhat incendiary (five years earlier, when Betty Hutton was romantically paired with Arturo

de Cordova in INCENDIARY BLONDE, several women's groups protested, and the movie was boycotted in Salt Lake City).

In MY MAN AND I, Montalban is a fruit picker named Chu Chu Ramirez. This time, the discrimination is specific. The hero is exploited by a Gringo con-man who cheats him out of his wages, then has him arrested. But though Ramirez becomes downhearted, he never loses faith in the American way, and even becomes a naturalized citizen to prove his patriotism. Peter Roffman and Jim Purdy's book *The Hollywood Social Problem Film* describes "Chu Chu's confidence that everything will work out. He is the standard friendly, happy Mexican whose faith in America is upheld when the injustice is rectified." Lucky it was rectified . . .

Montalban's image grew more serious with time, he improved as an actor and became a distinguished Hollywood activist for Hispanic rights, above all as founder of NOSOTROS. With his suave facade and innate dignity, he is a prime Hispanic role model and goodwill ambassador.

Fernando Lamas unfortunately never rose above his material, which invariably featured him as a devastating but caddish Latin playboy. Born in 1915, he made no Hollywood films until age 35. He arrived in California in 1950, and within a few years at MGM had a worldwide following. He did frivo-

Cesar Romero continued playing a variety of types

lous pictures like RICH, YOUNG AND PRETTY (1951) and partnered top actresses in THE MERRY WIDOW (1952, with Lana Turner), THE GIRL WHO HAD EVERYTHING (1953, with Elizabeth Taylor), DANGEROUS WHEN WET (1953, with Esther Williams, his fourth wife) and THE GIRL RUSH (1955, with Rosalind Russell).

In the late '50s, Lamas went into stage musicals like *The King and I* and demonstrated a fine singing voice. He thereafter alternated fewer films—some made in Europe—with nightclubs and directing for television. Before his death in 1982, he directed his son Lorenzo Lamas (by third wife Arlene Dahl), who achieved TV sex symboldom in "Falcon Crest," starring Jane Wyman, Ana-Alicia and Cesar Romero. (Lorenzo's birth had interrupted an episode of Wyman's 1950s TV series which Fernando was directing.)

By the '70s, as an actor, Lamas had transformed himself into "an all-around European character actor." In THE CHEAP DETECTIVE (1978), he played the Paul Henreid role from CASABLANCA, in the spy spoof written by Neil Simon. Lamas reasoned, "I did what was commercially sound. When in the '60s I saw that Latins were cast by the wayside, I developed an image as European. It was not hard for me to do, for I am handsome, Caucasian, and to

Dolores Del Rio and Maria Felix in LA CUCARACHA (1958)

In reality, Richard Martin had no accent. In *reel* life, Chito provided comic relief via his difficulty with English, although he was never a buffoon, and was the most subdued of any Western sidekick, Anglo or Hispanic. Chito's nationality was nebulous, but not his urge to dally with women, both of which the following screen exchange makes clear:

COWHAND: Say, Chito, you were pretty good with your dukes in that fight today.
CHITO: Oh, that was easy. That's the Irish in me.
TIM HOLT: Don't let him fool you. He's pretty good with the girls, too.
CHITO: Oh, that's easy, too. That's the Spanish in me.
COWHAND: Hey, now wait a minute. Are you an Irishman or a Mexican?
CHITO: I'm both—Chito Jose Gonzales Bustamonte Rafferty!

The ageless Dolores Del Rio

an American an accent is an accent—for all they know, you could be from Buenos Aires or Timbuktu!"

Posthumously, Lamas was immortalized by Billy Crystal on TV's "Saturday Night Live" as Fernando, the vain and charming foreign actor of indeterminate descent whose catch phrase was "You look mahvelous!"

Back on the Western front, there was one Hispanic cowboy sidekick who could have been the hero, but for his mangled English and intrinsically romantic nature. Richard "Chito" Martin appeared in more than 30 RKO Westerns through the 1940s and early '50s, most often paired with Tim Holt (in 29 films) but also Robert Mitchum and James Warren. Unlike cowboy sidekicks who were either shorter or heavier and inevitably funnier than the hero, Chito was handsomer than his partners.

Dolores Del Rio acted in early TV, opposite Cesar Romero and Chuck Connors

The once-popular Chito titles included UNDER THE TONTO RIM (1947), BROTHERS IN THE SADDLE (1949), DYNAMITE PASS (1950) and GUNPLAY (1951). In 1952, Richard Martin (born 1918) hung up his accent as Chito, for good. (Seven years later, he did turn up as a Mexican in FOUR FAST GUNS.)

Among the most daring of problem films in the '50s was THE LAWLESS (1950), helmed by Joseph Losey, a subsequent victim of political witch-hunts. The low-budget independent released through Paramount deals with fruit pickers, and their lives earning "six bits a day" for hard labor in the fields. Easier jobs are reserved for Anglos-only, and the Mexican workers can just afford meager "houses" without indoor plumbing, located "on the other side of the tracks."

As in WEST SIDE STORY, a community dance is invaded by white bigots who stir up trouble. The result: 11 Mexicans are arrested, and one Anglo. The press reports the violence as a battle between two gangs of "fruit tramps." Fighting the lies and

corruption via her small newspaper is Sunny (Gail Russell), who finds allies in certain liberal whites and tries to rouse her *compatriotas*, with varying degrees of success.

Upon its release, THE LAWLESS—whose title refers to the white community—was effectually ignored. (Its writer was Geoffrey Homes, a pseudonym for the blacklisted Daniel Mainwaring.) Years later, British *Photoplay* compared it to another pioneering problem film, THE SALT OF THE EARTH, directed by Herbert Biberman, one of the McCarthy era's Hollywood Ten.

"SALT is the more artistic of the two, and employs more Hispanic actors. It is also more black and white. Losey's movie recognizes that change is an ordeal which takes time, and that the future is unpredictable . . . Both movies offer the classic liberal antidote to racism and bigotry—unite and

I LOVE LUCY's Ethel and Lucy and Ricky (Ricardo, played by Desi Arnaz) and Fred

Young star Perry Lopez with Natalie Wood and Nick Adams

fight. But although Biberman's movie is based on a true incident, Losey's rings truer. Like life, it is problematic, on both sides."

More SALT, later.

Also more stereotypes, which offset many of the gains, for as cinema had increasingly to compete with television, stereotypes were again resorted to, in the names of thrills and dramatic chills. Witness the 1950 picture BRANDED, starring Alan Ladd as a blond anti-hero named Choya. After crossing the Mexican border, he battles an entire army of bandidos, then rescues and weds a rancher's daughter (Mona Freeman) who has been kidnapped by a "fiendish bandido"—played by Maltese actor Joseph Calleia, who often portrayed lawless Latins, as in MY LITTLE CHICKADEE (1940), with Mae West and W.C. Fields.

The 1952 CALIFORNIA CONQUEST offered dark-haired Cornel Wilde as a silk-suited, Spanish-blooded grandee who joins Fremont's "Freedom Forces" to defeat what one reviewer called "the greaser scum" of the Pacific state-to-be. In the process, he wins an Anglo bride (Teresa Wright) who tauntingly asks, "You *would* give a lot to be an American, wouldn't you?"

A 1952 horse of another color was VIVA ZAPATA!, written by John Steinbeck, directed by Elia Kazan

(*Here, and below*) Thomas Gomez
played varying nationalities of heavies

135

and starring Marlon Brando as Emiliano Zapata, the *campesino* (peasant) who became a Revolutionary hero and Mexican president. As Emiliano's brother Eufemio, Anthony Quinn won the first of two 1950s supporting Oscars, Jean Peters in dark makeup supplied the romantic interest, and Margo made a by-now infrequent appearance as one of Zapata's revolutionary comrades. The film, nominated for five Academy Awards, was a moderate success, though released at the height of McCarthyism.

Yet this film about the Mexican Revolution wasn't all that radical, for its basic message is that power corrupts. In order to retain his integrity, Zapata resigns from the presidency. He warns his people, "You've always looked for leaders, strong men without faults. There aren't any. There are no leaders but yourselves. They change. They desert. They die."

Mexican critics pointed out that the movie didn't even explain the Revolution's causes, and completely ignored the class conflicts at its root. Perhaps class conflict was too alarming a concept for a '50s film; Steinbeck even fashioned a pseudo-Marxist revolutionary dressed in villainous black named Fernando (Joseph Wiseman) who exhorts

Ricardo Montalban and Gilbert Roland in MARK OF THE RENEGADE (1951)

Zapata to sacrifice himself to the ongoing revolution. Once again, Hollywood betrayed its discomfort with any revolution less than 200 years old.

1953 offered more historical stereotypes. These would increase as the decade wore on and the Good Neighbor Policy faded from memory. Ramon Novarro explained, "The Latin image was starker, and the music and gaiety were forgotten as the war receded . . . There was less need not to offend former war allies, and television also had its bad influence, because the TV stereotypes encouraged the movies to return to stereotyping . . . I turned down many roles in which I would have played a villain or a caricature insulting to my own people.

"I used to joke with the producers, 'We ought to sue you for defamation of caricature.' They didn't think it was funny, or didn't get it."

In the 1953 MAN FROM THE ALAMO, Glenn Ford

Cary Grant in South America with Gilbert Roland in CRISIS (1950)

Gilbert Roland in THE BULLFIGHTER AND THE LADY (1951)

is a soldier ennobled by past association with the Alamo, that self-righteous symbol of white Texan history. Ford sets about "avenging the mass slaughter of frontier families by vicious renegades," according to *TV Guide*. Need one add that the victims are innocent Yankees and the vicious renegades *Mexicanos*?

RIDE VAQUERO! (1953) focused on its Hispanic villain—Anthony Quinn as José Esqueda—to a degree and with a force not seen in earlier bandido portraits. The MGM film's stars are Robert Taylor, Ava Gardner and Howard Keel, but Quinn steals the show. An article titled "The Mexican in the Movies" in *Screen Journal* characterized Esqueda as "a roistering cutthroat and braggart who uses brandy as a gargle, cavorts with 'gorls,' curses as strongly as mid-century censorship will permit, and connives to keep God-fearing Gringo settlers out of post-Civil War Texas by killing the men and raping the women."

Sounds grim, but *Time* felt that Quinn "provides the only glimpses of distinction and, at moments, is so good that he seems to have ridden into the scene out of some other movie." *The New York Times* called "Quinn's vigorous, colorful portrait of the chief culprit a pleasure to watch," while deriding the rest of the picture, including the against-type casting of Taylor as Quinn's lieutenant (named Rio). By fadeout, Esqueda and Rio have shot each other dead, leaving the disputed area in the hands of newlyweds Keel and Gardner. Entertaining, it may have been—to some—but progressive, it was not.

SALT OF THE EARTH (1954) is a near-legendary film. It was made by Herbert Biberman entirely outside the studio system, written by blacklisted Michael Wilson and produced by Paul Jarrico. Its inspiration was a real-life mining strike, and besides employing Hispanic actors like Juan Chacon and Rosaura Revueltas, SALT used the miners as actors; it was reportedly the first U.S.-made Hispanic-themed film to use mainly Hispanic actors. SALT also incorporated the historical background of white American industrialists' oppression of Chicanos and violation of their rights.

"We told the truth Hollywood didn't dare to tell," said Biberman.

In this case, the community owned the land, but when zinc was discovered, a corporation moved in, took over the property and offered the people a

Gilbert Roland in THE BIG CIRCUS (1959)

Mexican love goddess Elsa Aguirre

choice of moving elsewhere or taking jobs at rock-bottom wages. The natives are virtually indentured, indebted to the corporation in whose shabby houses they live and at whose stores they shop for overpriced goods which they are encouraged to buy on credit.

SALT also spotlights the lack of safety standards for Mexican-Americans, who must perform dangerous tasks singly, while Anglo miners may work in pairs. When the former finally protest, the Anglo manager retorts that he can easily replace them. "With who? A scab?" asks an angry Chicano. "With an *American*," snaps the manager.

Hailed by some as the most daring social problem film ever, SALT was criticized by others for painting its white characters too black. If so—and bearing in mind that it was based on reality—it was time for a cinematic turnabout. And while the evolution of passive miners into passionate strikers is rather rapid, it is mandated by the film's limited running time. The happy ending, though glib, is a

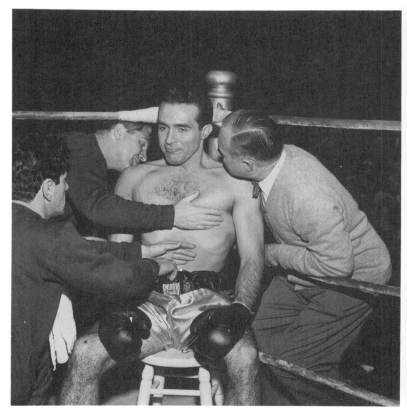

Ricardo Montalban as a boxer in RIGHT CROSS (1950), co-starring June Allyson

welcome alternative to a finale of dead or hopeless Hispanics.

Extremely controversial, SALT OF THE EARTH was sabotaged by being unofficially ignored—by distributors and by most of the media. It was quietly banned from most venues, and kept out of circulation until well after the McCarthy period. Even today, it is almost never seen on television. An anonymous Hispanic executive at a major Los Angeles TV station noted, "I looked into getting the rights to air it, but management said it was too inflammatory, especially with our large Latino community here . . . Sometimes the truth is frightening."

In 1958, it was back to that ultimate greaser type, Pancho Villa, with Rodolfo Hoyos in VILLA! The cruel and surly bandit who murders and then steals from the rich and keeps the loot for himself also accumulates a harem of "wives" meant to stimulate audience interest in a tired subject. (Hoyos' Villa at least made more sense than Yul Brynner's in the 1968 VILLA RIDES, directed by Sam Peckinpah. One

Marlon Brando in VIVA ZAPATA! (1952)

142

Katy Jurado looking on in Mexico, top left

critic complained, "Brynner spends most of the movie adjusting a lop-sided wig and staring at the audience.")

Coronet magazine compared Hoyos with Gilbert Roland, who starred in the 1955 TREASURE OF PANCHO VILLA, which was not about Villa but the treasure he left behind. "Roland is a more charming evil-doer than Hoyos, whose authenticity in the

Katy Jurado looked upon in Mexico, shortly before Hollywood called

part is oppressively heavy. The character's deeds demand his demise by fadeout, but Roland's convincing accent proves delightful, and the sparkle in his roguish eyes contrasts favorably with the lethargic yet vicious enactment of the Hispanic actor." *Coronet* apparently thought that Roland was not Hispanic and could therefore give a better performance!

Critic Wyatt Cooper believed, "The real Pancho Villa is likely lost to us, his dusty memory buried in the sand dunes of one Hollywood biopic after another . . . Why he should be the most popular Latino character in Hollywood history is a mystery." Or is it? Hoyos later told the Argentine newspaper *La Prensa*, "What Villa supplies to North American audiences is drama and danger, the 'reality' of a historical personage, and a scapegoat who comes to a terrible and violent end."

Anthony Quinn again stole the show in the 1955 SEVEN CITIES OF GOLD, about explorer Gaspar de Portola (Quinn) and Father Junipero Serra (Michael Rennie) in late-1700s California. *Time* announced, "Best of all is Quinn, who wears the conquering swagger of Castile like one to that overbearing manner born." Richard Egan played a less convincing Spaniard, Jose Mendoza, and Jeffrey Hunter and Rita Moreno played Indian "savages." When Rita as Ula is seduced by Egan, she leaps off a cliff to her death, out of cinematic shame. Egan later admitted, "Quinn and Moreno would *have* to come across better than me or Rennie or Hunter; none of us had any business playing Spaniards *or* Indians!" Perhaps *Time*'s commendation to Quinn signified mainstream realization that Hispanic and Spanish characters are best played by actors with the appropriate backgrounds.

Quinn in 1956 was THE MAN FROM DEL RIO, taking center stage as Dave Robles, a Mexican gunman

Mario "Cantinflas" Moreno, the "Mexican Chaplin"

whose quick-draw earns him the badge of sheriff in a frightened Texas border town called Mesa. As sheriff, Robles feels he is at last being given his share of dignity by the bigoted Anglo Texans. However, when he dresses up specially to attend the community's church social, he is shunned as a Mexican. Even Estella (Katy Jurado) rebuffs him, in the best tradition of the "dark lady" who prefers Anglo lovers.

Robles is one of Quinn's favorite roles: "The man has a tenacity and spirit that can't be broken, by other people or his own, and in the end he proves himself braver and more stubborn than any of his oppressors." Robles, while suffering from a broken wrist, takes on the town's chief bigot in a shootout. The latter loses but survives, and is sent packing by Robles.

Time's review was questionable, to say the least. ". . . By scratching, bumbling, slobbering and gaz-

145

Cantinflas in AROUND THE WORLD IN 80 DAYS (1956)

tion by the U.S. army against Villa. The film starred Gary Cooper, and Rita Hayworth as a non-Hispanic who provides the dramatic highpoint when Cooper's men—Tab Hunter, Dick York, Richard Conte, Van Heflin and Michael Callan—try to rape the prisoner before Captain Cooper steps in, in the nick of time. The relatively unambitious Rita Hayworth claimed that throughout her career she never yearned to play any particular role, save one:

"I would have liked to play Federico Garcia Lorca's 'Yerma,' the story of a barren woman who has no children and whose husband rejects her. It's a tremendous part, and the few times I mentioned an

Spain's leading star, Sarita Montiel, who worked briefly in Hollywood in the 1950s

Sarita Montiel

ing dumbly out of his unshaven face, Quinn manages to make a conventional pasteboard character seem like a real human slob."

There was a minor outcry when Orson Welles cast Charlton Heston as Mexican Ramon Vargas in his 1958 A TOUCH OF EVIL. Welles improbably explained, "The public is used to seeing this sort of thing." The *Los Angeles Herald Examiner* stated, "This story could have been set anywhere, but uses a Mexican border town for foreign color. Why, then, the casting of the very Saxon and thoroughly wooden Heston as a Mexican cop? . . . Perhaps we should be grateful that Heston hasn't thus far shown up as that most dastardly, oft-chronicled Mexican, Pancho Villa."

THEY CAME TO CORDURA (1959) dealt indirectly with Villa. Specifically, with a 1916 punitive expedi-

José Ferrer, the first Hispanic actor to win an Oscar

Arturo De Cordova returned to Mexico after Hollywood underused him; seen here in FRUTO PROHIBIDO (Forbidden Fruit, 1952)

During the '50s, Rita Moreno (here with Tom Ewell in THE LIEUTENANT WORE
SKIRTS, 1956) marked time . . .

Burt Lancaster, Gary Cooper and Sarita Montiel in VERA CRUZ (1954)

interest in it, while I was still the right age, the people with whom I discussed it said they had never heard of it."

But the decade's most popular movie with a Hispanic reference was George Stevens' 1956 GIANT, starring Elizabeth Taylor, Rock Hudson and James Dean. Its Texas love triangle is set against the struggle for economic supremacy between entrenched cattle men and oil men. A subplot touches on the struggle between Anglos and Hispanics (played by Sal Mineo and a handful of "unknown" actors). Though the sprawling and leisurely picture dotes on its Anglo stars and themes, its ending, which involves intermarriage, is significant.

It makes clear, via the resultant offspring, that the future will have to be shared by groups of people living and working, and sometimes loving, together. Like SALT OF THE EARTH, its ultimate message is that the oppressed can only change their lot when they face the majority on an equal footing and cultivate pride in their past, present and future.

Sarita Montiel and Gary Cooper in VERA CRUZ

Katy Jurado and Gary Cooper in HIGH NOON
(1952)

"Spitfire" Rita Moreno

Director John Huston and José Ferrer as Toulouse-Lautrec in
THE MOULIN ROUGE (1952)

(*Here, and on facing page*) Marlon Brando as Emiliano Zapata in VIVA ZAPATA (1952), below with director Elia Kazan and Jean Peters

Anthony Quinn and Marlon Brando in VIVA ZAPATA!

Rita Hayworth in THEY CAME TO CORDURA (1959)

Katy Jurado
and Cesar Romero

Katy Jurado

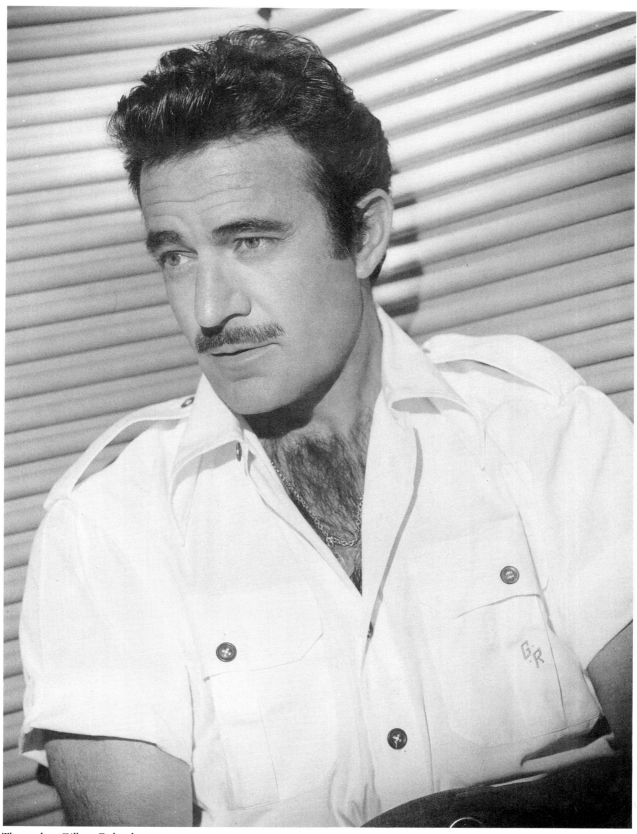

The ageless Gilbert Roland

5. THE SIXTIES:
Alien Nation?

"The 1960s was important for social movements and for progress. But for Hollywood, it was a horrible time! The glamour was gone, the good writers were gone, the good women's roles were gone . . . But most of all, *we* were gone!"
—Dolores Del Rio to the author, 1979

The '60s began and ended with two contrasting but strictly non-Hispanic views of that historic symbol of Mexican-American divisiveness, the Alamo. In THE ALAMO (1960), starring, produced and directed by John Wayne, history was rewritten to glorify the American settlers who wrested Texas from Mexico. Yet again, a handful of idealistic Yankees triumphs—for a time, in this case—over a horde of violent, inept Latins, and the Latina is again depicted more sympathetically (in the person of Argentine Linda Cristal) than male Latinos. Not surprisingly, the largest roles went to the Anglo protagonists, including Wayne as Davy Crockett, Richard Widmark as James Bowie, Laurence Harvey as William Travis and Richard Boone as Sam Houston.

The story of Santa Anna's 1836 storming of the Alamo garrison in San Antonio de Bexar was reshaped according to Hollywood habit and Wayne's right-wing leanings. The inaccurate film—partly directed by an uncredited John Ford—shows Wayne's Crockett fighting to the bitter end (just as all the screen Crocketts before him), when in fact it's unknown whether Crockett died fighting or was shot after surrendering to the Mexicans. In the celluloid ALAMO, Bowie is a very active joint commander with Travis; in reality, Bowie was too sick to fight, and issued orders from his bed.

THE ALAMO depicts Houston worrying over the possible fate of the Alamo. In fact, he'd already ordered Bowie to blow it up and withdraw the garrison. Also, the movie dramatically portrays Travis

(*On facing page*) Anthony Quinn and "Indian" Anjanette Comer in GUNS FOR SAN SEBASTIAN

George Maharis and Wende Wagner in A COVENANT WITH DEATH (1966)

offending Bowie over a recent letter from Bowie's wife. In actuality, she'd died years before! These are only the major fallacies. As the Chilean magazine *Puntos de Vista* (Points of View) put it, "In its epic disregard for history or fairness, and in its myriad misrepresentative details, THE ALAMO is nothing more than a famous site and battle shamelessly transformed into nationalistic propaganda."

When it came time to stump for Academy Award nominations, John Wayne, whose company co-owned the film (which co-starred two of his off-spring), ran an ultra-patriotic ad campaign. It even went so far as to suggest, in movie industry trade journals, that to not cast a vote for THE ALAMO would be downright un-American.

At odds with the almost religiously solemn THE ALAMO was the farcical 1969 VIVA MAX, about the modern-day retaking of the Alamo by a bumblingly inept, allegedly hilarious Mexican general. The sort who could easily be outsmarted by a Gringo child. Peter Ustinov, who a decade later raised Oriental hackles with his one-dimensional Charlie Chan portrayal, inspired minor demonstrations in larger cities where VIVA MAX played.

Ustinov's oily, corrupt, incompetent buffoon general led one Hispanic-American critic to suggest, "We should sue the moviemakers for defamation of character." This writer's mother, whose father was a non-*reel* Mexican general, sent numerous protest letters to the producer and to cinemas which ran the offending film.

THE ALAMO nearly bankrupted John Wayne, but eventually earned a small profit. VIVA MAX was a less costly film, but drew even fewer American patrons (and was banned in a few Latin countries). Both movies insulted Hispanics, but perhaps the latter also alienated mainstream audiences who believed "Remember the Alamo!" wasn't a theme intended for comic treatment.

By another token, Cantinflas, Latin America's top comic actor and the Spanish-speaking world's foremost box office attraction, didn't fare well by

Linda Christian and Miguel Mateo Miguelin in THE MOMENT OF TRUTH (1964)

Hollywood or in the U.S. market. Four years after the huge success of AROUND THE WORLD IN 80 DAYS, Hollywood took a second look at Cantinflas, and in 1960 fashioned PEPE as a movie vehicle for him. An all-star supporting cast was employed as added insurance, but Cantinflas played—once more—a glorified manual, who got to pine for the blonde Americana (Shirley Jones) but didn't come close to bedding, let alone wedding, her. Instead, at fadeout, Cantinflas is reunited with his beloved horse, whom he calls "my son."

PEPE's top-heavy cast included Cesar Romero, whose '60s roles declined in quantity and quality in films like SEVEN WOMEN FROM HELL (1961), TWO

Pedro Armendariz passed away in the 1960s

Pedro Armendariz and Heidi Bruhl in CAPTAIN SINDBAD (1963)

ON A GUILLOTINE (1964) and SERGEANT DEAD-HEAD (1965). He got to play a more interesting and active role in A TALENT FOR LOVING (1969), as a Mexican landowner who tricks footloose Richard Widmark into marrying one of his daughters— each of whom has a talent for loving. However, in the mid-1960s Romero discovered a whole new generation of fans and a wider stardom than ever as the Joker in TV's campy "Batman." The series' popularity revived in the late 1980s with the tremendous success of the film version starring Jack Nicholson as another, darker Joker.

Other Hispanic stars had to leave Hollywood for Europe, to continue in lead roles at a time when Hollywood increasingly stressed "whitebread" personalities. By the 1960s, the only foreign nationality still "in" was British—and how!—musically and in pictures. In Italy, Ricardo Montalban starred in PIRATE WARRIOR (1961) as the Black Pirate, a good guy fighting to end slavery in "San Salvador." Back in a Hollywood film (shot as the French Riviera), he played an impoverished European duke in LOVE IS A BALL (1963), a Glenn Ford vehicle. Montalban finished the decade as an Italian movie heartthrob in Shirley MacLaine's SWEET CHARITY.

Fernando Lamas fared less well. He began the decade with science-fiction, in THE LOST WORLD (1960), then played swashbucklers in Italian cheapie epics before turning, late in the decade, to eminently forgettable TV films such as the aptly titled THE LONELY PROFESSION (1969). Gilbert Roland also found that being a Hispanic actor in Hollywood was a lonely and part-time profession— he made only four films in that decade which preferred such actors to have either no accent or an anglicized name, or both (like Anthony Quinn, as we shall see).

Roland's best '60s role was a stoic Cheyenne

Cantinflas in PEPE (1960)

Mexican superstar Cantinflas

Karl Malden and Marlon Brando in ONE-EYED JACKS (1960)

leader in John Ford's first pro-Indian Western (his last Western, too), CHEYENNE AUTUMN (1964). It co-starred Montalban and Dolores Del Rio as the "Spanish" mother of Indian brave Sal Mineo. The tragic story of the U.S. government's broken promises to and sadistic persecution of a given tribe was again dominated by Anglo actors, including Richard Widmark, James Stewart, Edward G. Robinson and the very blonde Carroll Baker. One of AUTUMN's most chillingly illustrated truths is the bleeding of a minority's strength once its members turn against each other, thereby playing into their oppressors' hands—embodied by the murder of Mineo by Montalban.

Dolores Del Rio's first Hollywood film since the '40s was the 1960 Elvis Presley vehicle FLAMING STAR, in which she played the star's mother in a story about amorous Indian-American relations. "In Hollywood, so many of us played [Native Americans], if we worked there at all. For, Westerns were very popular in the 1960s, and the few Hispanic characters in Hollywood were often played by Hollywood stars. Even less suitable ones like Paul Newman or Janet Leigh," recalled Del Rio in 1979.

(Puerto Rican-American Chita Rivera played Dick Van Dyke's secretary girlfriend on Broadway in BYE BYE, BIRDIE. But when Hollywood transferred the hit musical to film in 1963, they cast Janet Leigh as Rose De Leon opposite Van Dyke, fitting

Yul Brynner and sextet in RETURN OF THE SEVEN (1966)

Peter Ustinov in VIVA MAX!

169

Hollywood newcomer Raquel Welch emotes

Raquel Welch opposite John Richardson, Edward G. Robinson and Dean Martin

her into a "Mexican wig." The talented Rivera, who has appeared in only a couple of films, had to wait till 1969 for a juicy, albeit supporting screen role as a dancehall hostess in SWEET CHARITY.)

After mothering teen favorites Presley and Mineo, the agelessly beautiful Del Rio returned to Mexico to work on screen and on the stage, appearing at 63 in the romantic title role of the play THE LADY OF THE CAMELLIAS in Mexico City. She eventually accepted a glamourous cameo role in the international co-production MORE THAN A MIRACLE, a 1967 fairy tale top-billing Sophia Loren and Omar Sharif.

Katy Jurado also began the '60s in Hollywood

support, in ONE-EYED JACKS, a thunderous flop whose publicity dwelt on the stormy affair between Marlon Brando (who also directed) and leading lady Pina Pellicer (discovered in Mexico City), who committed suicide once the affair ended. After unchallenging features like A COVENANT WITH DEATH (1967), starring George Maharis, Jurado moved into television films.

1961 saw the release of two differing films about the war between urban Hispanic gangs and their paler counterparts. The less commercially successful picture was THE YOUNG SAVAGES, starring Burt Lancaster as an assistant D.A. initially seeking the

Anthony Quinn as the legendary Leon Alastray in GUNS FOR SAN SEBASTIAN (1968)

"Indians" Charles Bronson (right) and Jaime Hernandez in GUNS FOR SAN SEBASTIAN

death penalty for the murderers of a blind Puerto Rican youth. The movie was shot in its actual setting, New York's Spanish Harlem, and was based on true events.

Escalante, the blind boy, was a member of an upper east side gang, the Horsemen, whose chief rivals are the T-Birds, an Italian gang. One afternoon, three T-Birds stab Escalante, who is later revealed to have pimped for his sister, a prostitute. Lancaster delves into the case, and pins the murder on a T-Bird whose mother (Shelley Winters) Lancaster had dated before marrying Dina Merrill. The film wastes time and star-power on the uninteresting love triangle, but does manage to denounce the Italian-Americans' anti-Hispanic racism. Cultural clashes abound, as when a non-Hispanic at the public swimming pool taunts a Puerto Rican wearing a crucifix, "I thought only girls wore necklaces . . ."

The New York Times complained, "The problems of juvenile delinquency are tough enough to cope with these days, but a film that sees the problems and then soft-soaps them, doesn't provide much valid drama or do much good." Partly because of Ms. Winters, Lancaster decides not to pursue a death penalty for the primary murderer, who is found guilty of third-degree assault and sentenced to a year in a boys' prison at Elmira, for "evaluation and rehabilitation."

Winters' character is grateful, but the Puerto Rican mother (Pilar Seurat) demands of Lancaster, "Where is the justice for a dead blind boy? What about the animals who killed my son?" The assistant D.A., who has learned much about bigotry via this case, sadly utters the film's last line: "A lot of people killed your son, Mrs. Escalante."

A less gritty, even poetic view of teenage gangs was served up in the Oscar-winning musical WEST

SIDE STORY. This updating of the classic Romeo and Juliet story featured an Anglo Romeo (Richard Beymer) and a Puerto Rican Juliet—the non-Hispanic Natalie Wood, whose singing voice was dubbed and whose speaking accent helped earn her the Hasty Pudding Club's award for worst actress of the year.

Ironically, WSS did earn an Academy Award for Puerto Rican Rita Moreno as Maria's brother's girl Anita. "Somebody in Hollywood came up with the brilliant idea of casting a Puerto Rican in a Puerto Rican part!" explained Moreno, to date the sole Hispanic actress to win an Oscar. Nonetheless, another supporting Academy Award went to Greek-American George Chakiris, the actor-dancer who played Wood's brother. Despite the musical's tremendous success, neither performer went on to movie stardom, and in 1963 Chakiris played a Mayan king in the costly flop KINGS OF THE SUN, co-starring Yul Brynner.

By the time she won her historic Oscar, Moreno had completed her fiery Latina turn in the film of SUMMER AND SMOKE. Her new-found prestige gave her the courage to avoid Hollywood for most of the rest of the decade:

"It wasn't easy. I was terrified at first. I knew I had to get out of town because there was too much temptation here. I could have taken any of those spitfire roles and made a bundle. Luckily, I was so demeaned—it's really demeaning after you've won the Oscar to be offered the same role over and over again. They only wanted me to drag out my accent-and-dance show over and over again. And boy, I was offered them all—gypsy fortune-tellers, Mexican spitfires, Spanish spitfires, Puerto Ricans—all those 'Yonkee peeg, you steal me people's money' parts.

"The only thing I could do was turn my back on it." Which she did until 1968, when Marlon Brando cast her as his leading lady in THE NIGHT OF THE FOLLOWING DAY, as a character simply called *Blonde*. (In the early '60s, after *their* affair had ended, Moreno tried to commit suicide in Brando's living room.) Unfortunately, NIGHT bombed.

WEST SIDE STORY, like YOUNG SAVAGES, soft-pedalled the anti-racist message until its dramatic conclusion, in which Maria's Anglo lover is murdered, as was her brother. Most of the picture blends romance—again between non-Hispanic

Dolores Del Rio and Sal Mineo in CHEYENNE AUTUMN (1964)

stars—and balletic gang warfare showcasing Leonard Bernstein's spectacular score. But WSS' popularity did open the door to more screen depictions of urban Hispanics' lives, even though usually in gangs or other equally violent circumstances.

One letter to *The New York Times* stated, "As a Puerto Rican immigrant, I applaud the dignified and even-handed portrayal of my countrymen in this big-budget movie. At the same time, I am disappointed that most Americans, who may never

focused anyway on blacks and Sidney Poitier. "The problem," Fernando Lamas told Johnny Carson, "is that we don't have a Latin Sidney Poitier. . ."

Thus, Paul Newman starred as bandit Juan Carrasco in THE OUTRAGE, the 1964 film of Fay and Michael Kanin's play based on Akira Kurosawa's classic RASHOMON. The setting was changed from feudal Japan to the late 19th century Old West, but a pair of Britishers, Claire Bloom and Laurence Harvey, enacted the raped wife and the murdered husband. Newman, who still considers Carrasco one of his best performances, went to Mexico to

view another movie with Puerto Rican characters, mostly have to judge us from the performances of non-Puerto Ricans, particularly in most of the important speaking roles."

The trend of casting non-Hispanics was exacerbated in the 1960s by the paucity of good or sizeable Hispanic roles. With censorship finally relaxed, Hollywood was more attracted to themes of newly available sex and violence than social problem films about minorities, most of which

Gilbert Roland and Dolores Del Rio in CHEYENNE AUTUMN

Carroll Baker, Dolores Del Rio and Gilbert Roland in CHEYENNE AUTUMN

research his part, reportedly studying manners, customs and the language of the local citizenry.

Judith Crist wrote in the *New York Herald Tribune*, "Newman emerges as a junior-grade Leo Carrillo, spitting and spewing and wallowing in dialect and playing the villain, the lecher, the social outcast, the lover and the coward to the hilt." A fiasco, THE OUTRAGE has today all but vanished, even from TV.

Hollywood had transplanted another Kurosawa classic, SEVEN SAMURAI, to the generic Old West in 1960, as THE MAGNIFICENT SEVEN, starring Yul Brynner, Steve McQueen, Charles Bronson and four other non-Hispanic heroes defending a helpless Mexican village against villains led by "Mexican bandit" Eli Wallach, in a performance resurrecting all the old greaser characteristics, and a role he would reprise in a number of Italian and Spanish-made action films. The film was an enormous hit, and marked the big-time Hollywood bow of Mexican actress Rosenda Monteros (she had been in several Mexican-made "Hollywood" movies earlier, including VILLA! in 1958.) However, one

Gilbert Roland in the mid-'60s, with and minus mustache

of McQueen's biographers described her "bally-hooed American debut" as "only a nod in the direction of the Mexican government." In any event, Monteros' last major English-language film was the 1965 SHE, in which she played second female lead to Ursula Andress.

Brynner starred in the 1966 sequel THE RETURN OF THE SEVEN, declaring, "I believe in this film. It's about a noble band of adventurers rescuing Mexican peasants who are being used as slave labor." Still, with the helpless Mexican peasants and their

Dolores Del Rio

Hollywood's most visible non-blonde sex symbol since fellow *Hispana* Rita Hayworth. Like Hayworth, Welch's talent improved with time, but the feistier Welch developed into a multi-media survivor.

The 1964 film THE NIGHT OF THE IGUANA, from Tennessee Williams' play, exemplified another deepening cosmetic trend: using Latin locations for their exoticism (and cheap extras) while sticking to stories involving non-Hispanic characters. In the '60s, Hollywood went on location as never before, mostly to Europe but sometimes to Latin America and particularly Mexico, especially in Westerns (THE MAGNIFICANT SEVEN was shot near Cuernavaca). John Huston chose the sleepy fishing village of Puerto Vallarta for IGUANA, in which Ava Gardner runs a hilltop hotel peopled by, among others, Richard Burton and Deborah Kerr.

IGUANA's Mexican speaking parts (all bit parts) were three—a bartender (Emilio "El Indio" Fernandez) and Pepe (Fidelmar Duran) and Pedro (Robert Leyva), the servants-cum-beach boys with

noble rescuers! In 1968, Brynner was Pancho Villa in VILLA RIDES (made in Spain, where else?). The picture, panned by Hispanics and critics alike, bypassed Latin actors for leading and secondary roles; Charles Bronson played Fierro, "the butcher of the Revolution," and Herbert Lom was General Huerta. On location, Brynner told reporters, "The one negative thing about stories with Latins in them is that there is so much violence. But you do have to give the public what it wants." Or was it more a question of what Hollywood preferred to dish out?

Raquel Welch (neé Tejada in 1940) made her inauspicious screen debut in A HOUSE IS NOT A HOME (1964), but two years later she made an impact in the sci-fi hit FANTASTIC VOYAGE, then cemented her fame with the British ONE MILLION YEARS, B.C., clad in designer cavewoman garb. Not Hispanic-identified until the 1980s, she shuttled from one B-grade film to another, but remained

Dolores Del Rio as Elvis Presley's mother in FLAMING STAR (1960)

178

Ursula Andress, Elvis Presley and Elsa Cardenas have FUN IN ACAPULCO (1963)

Reginald Gardiner, Eve Arden, Cesar Romero and Gale Gordon in SERGEANT DEADHEAD (1965)

179

BYE BYE BIRDIE's Dick Van Dyke and Janet Leigh, who played Rose De Leon in the 1963 film

SWEET CHARITY (1969) starred Paula Kelly, Shirley MacLaine and Chita Rivera (who'd played BYE BYE BIRDIE's Rose De Leon on Broadway)

whom Ava spends passionate hours in the moonlit surf of Mismaloya Beach, today a tourist attraction. Indeed, the town itself became a tourist magnet after worldwide publicity centered on the romantic escapades there of Burton and Elizabeth Taylor, who later bought adjoining homes in the resort.

Then again, sometimes the U.S. doubled for Mexico, as in THE PROFESSIONALS (1966), shot on the U.S. side of the Mexican border but set in Texas and 1917 Mexico. The title refers to four Americans (Burt Lancaster, Lee Marvin, Robert Ryan and Woody Strode) hired by railroad tycoon Ralph Bellamy to rescue his young Mexican wife Maria (Italian Claudia Cardinale), who has supposedly been

Mel Ferrer as EL GRECO (1964)

Omar Sharif as Che Guevara in CHE! (1969)

kidnapped by Mexican revoluntionary Jesus Raza (Jack Palance!). Along the way to Raza's stronghold, the quartet kill off untold Mexicans like so many flies, until Lancaster finally captures Raza— who has had sex with the very willing Maria.

In a surprising twist, Lancaster and Raza/Palance share a cigar and fond memories of the Revolution's early days. When the real kidnapper turns out to be Bellamy himself, the four Americans, having lost their $10,000 reward, join up with Raza, a three-dimensional character as written, and as played by

181

Omar Sharif and Jack Palance (as Fidel Castro) in CHE!

the "less than suitable" but talented Palance. Together, like five musketeers, they all head for the Mexican Revolution!

The following year saw the passing, from a stroke, of the venerable Antonio Moreno, Hollywood's first Spanish or Hispanic star. Few remembered that in the mid-1920s, best-selling novelist Elinor Glyn, "Hollywood's high priestess of allure," had averred that "only a chosen few" had *It*, a code word for the then-taboo phrase "sex appeal." To a fascinated nation, she revealed the fab four who had *It*—"Antonio Moreno, Rex the Wild Stallion, a doorman at the Ambassador Hotel, and Clara Bow." Bow went on to stardom as "the *It* Girl," but Moreno, already a star, didn't need a gimmick or *It*-identification.

In 1968, Moreno was followed by Ramon Novarro, brutally murdered by two hustler brothers who ransacked his Hollywood home for the plentiful cash they'd heard he kept there. Though

(*Here, and on facing page*) Scenes from THE ALAMO (1960), which starred John Wayne, Richard Widmark, Laurence Harvey and Linda Cristal

wealthy and retired from the screen, Novarro was a movie buff who kept up with the latest releases, having long since installed his own private cinema. In 1967, he'd told *Show* magazine, "I love the United States of America, and I love living here.

"But as an actor and as an individual, I find myself in a dual position. Like others from Latin America, I am part of an alien nation within a larger nation . . . The fruits of our labor are prized and needed, but we are kept apart, due to our language and culture. They like our food and admire our colorful art, but do not accept us as peers. Even in Hollywood, and not even after decades of positive change in other arenas."

The proof of Hollywood's ethno-political stagnation was the casting of Jack Palance in a secondary Mexican role in a film already loaded with box office names. Yul Brynner could have been talking about Hispanic actors when he referred, after THE KING AND I, to Hollywood's casting Caucasians as Orientals. "They don't trust Oriental actors being talented enough to play their own characters . . . Hollywood's outstanding characteristic, after greed, has always been arrogance."

Paul Newman as a Mexican bandit in THE OUTRAGE (1964)

In the '60s, Anthony Quinn moved away from his quasi-Latin image after two '50s supporting Oscars and subsequent participation in numerous prestige pictures, typically as non-Hispanics—non-Americans, too. Though he sued Yul Brynner for $500,000 after being excluded from THE MAGNIFICENT SEVEN, Quinn had a parallel 1961 hit with THE GUNS OF NAVARONE. (Quinn apparently had been promised a co-starring role—probably the one played by Eli Wallach—and reportedly became even more annoyed when THE MAGNIFICENT SEVEN turned into such a smash.) He then played Arab in LAWRENCE OF ARABIA, Spanish in BEHOLD A PALE HORSE, mittel-European in THE VISIT (all 1964), and became an honorary Greek after the critical and popular hit ZORBA THE GREEK (1964). Quinn did not play the ethnically suitable role of Mexican-Irish ALVAREZ KELLY in 1966; William Holden did.

But he returned to the fold in 1968 in GUNS FOR SAN SEBASTIAN, as the legendary Mexican outlaw-patriot Leon Alastray. This time it was colonial Mexicans vs. American Indians (the Yaquis, played by Charles Bronson, Anjanette Comer, etc.). Hunted by Spanish government troops in 1746 Mexico, Alastray takes refuge in a church run by an old priest (Sam Jaffe!). When he escapes, he disguises himself as a cleric and heads for the town of San Sebastian, where he's hailed as a spiritual leader and an ally against the ever-attacking Yaquis.

Anthony Quinn with Marcus Ohrner in THE 25TH HOUR (1967)

184

Anna Magnani and Anthony Quinn in THE SECRET OF SANTA VITTORIA (1969)

Alastray encourages the townspeople to rebuild their dam, and secures much-needed guns and ammunition for them via his ex-mistress Silvia Pinal, now married to the local governor. After aiding San Sebastian in their victory, Alastray is recognized by a visiting army captain, and again manages to flee toward a sure-to-be-adventurous future.

After SAN SEBASTIAN, Quinn completed the decade with further variegated performances, including a Russian pope in THE SHOES OF THE FISHERMAN and an Italian wine enthusiast in THE SECRET OF SANTA VITTORIA. Only with the 1970s did he begin to slow down and have to turn increasingly to European productions, returning to Hollywood in a big way in 1978 as THE GREEK TYCOON (a

very thinly disguised Aristotle Onassis). He didn't make a Spanish-language film until 1982's VALENTINA.

BANDOLERO! (1968) was another made-in-Texas story which starts out in the U.S. but quickly heads south, the better to include easy violence, made-to-order villains and "local color." The movie stars Dean Martin, Raquel Welch and James Stewart, and concerns bank robbers fleeing the law and thus wending their way to Mexico, "the territory of the bandolero," where Yankees both outlaw and in-law are apt to be killed by bullet-crazed locals. The picture ends in a bloodbath, and one critic noted, "Americans holding off Mexicans in a scene of grim carnage was not new to the set of the film; the director used the same buildings near Bracketville, Texas, that John Wayne had used in THE ALAMO."

By decade's end, the stereotypes were coming fast and thick, and the violence had escalated. THE GOOD, THE BAD AND THE UGLY came galloping along in 1967, with Clint Eastwood as the Good (named Blondy), Lee Van Cleef as the Bad, and Eli Wallach as the Ugly—Wallach as Tuco reprising his shifty, bloodthirsty "greaser." The Mexican Tuco has somehow found his way up north during the American Civil War, where he and his two gold-seeking associates wreak havoc that however palls next to the organized mass slaughter carried out by both sides of the war. "I've never seen so many men wasted so badly," says Blondy, but the picture ends with a three-way gunfight.

By the late '60s, the Hispanic community was more vocal and united, but protests to studios had no effect when the movies in question were money-makers. And because Latin governments had practically stopped addressing Hollywood, it was all up to Hispanic-Americans and their organizations, which would gather strength in the coming decades . . .

In 1969, two non-Hispanic actors played Latin roles of a different sort, in an unusual—especially for Hollywood—venture. CHE! starred Omar

Anthony Quinn as a Spanish federale in BEHOLD A PALE HORSE (1964)

Margaret O'Brien, Eileen Heckart, Anthony Quinn and Sophia Loren in HELLER IN PINK TIGHTS (1960)

THE FIREBRAND (1962) starred Valentin De Vargas as Joaquin Murieta

Sharif, an Egyptian Muslim (born Michel Shalhoub, a Lebanese Christian), as revolutionary Che Guevara, with Jack Palance—again—as Fidel Castro. The *Los Angeles Herald Examiner* called the flop "a new low for Hollywood, trying to upgrade Castro's image via the debatably heroic Guevara, with the most unimaginable stars in both roles! . . . Almost as inane are the gratuitous violence and murky plotline."

But the film which drew the most criticism for excess violence was THE WILD BUNCH (1969), directed by Sam "blood 'n gore" Peckinpah. This time out, most everybody dies in the end, including the title anti-heroes, robbers played by William Holden, Ernest Borgnine, Warren Oates, Ben Johnson and, yes, Jaime Sanchez as Angel, a Mexican who feels close to "my people, my village—Mexico." Therefore, after their foiled robbery, Angel persuades the aging outlaws to escape to Mexico, where they settle in his village for a brief, scenic respite before the resumption of the violence that permeates the picture.

On the one hand, Peckinpah, Warner Bros. and Hollywood were blamed for the insensate amount and degree of violence, i.e., a horse stomping on a woman and dragging a man through the dirt, bodies falling in slow motion with blood spurting out of them (but only after being shot and remaining standing past all belief), etc. One of the movie's special effects experts claimed that more ammunition was used to make THE WILD BUNCH than was used in the Mexican Revolution, some 90,000 rounds!

Peckinpah defended his "ballets of death" as being no worse than what one saw on the nightly news of the war in Vietnam, but the film elicited strong reactions, then and now. Many critics dismissed it as "mindless trash" or "an evil influence." Author Jay Hyams called it "one of the most important Westerns ever made and one of the most important American films ever made." Apart from its intrinsic bloodletting and whoring scenes, THE WILD BUNCH does have some strongpoints:

It offers a sometimes poetic portrait of the death of the Old West. The story takes place in 1913, by which time the Western frontier has closed, and aging outlaws with their guns and rough individualism are hemmed in by technology—particularly motorcars and machine guns—and growing groups of people and institutions. Loyalty is the

187

(Here, and on facing page) Scenes from the Oscar-winning WEST SIDE STORY (1961), starring Natalie Wood, Richard Beymer, Rita Moreno and George Chakiris

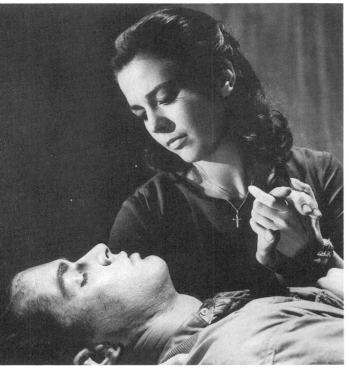

Wild Bunch's credo, their method of survival and retaining their dignity. As Holden says, "When you side with a man, you side with him all the way—otherwise you're an animal." The villainy is here evenly distributed, among industry (again represented by a railroad magnate) and callous bounty hunters north of the border, and fanatical anti-Revolutionists south of it. Violence, *sí*, stereotypes, *no*.

The motley Bunch is unswervingly loyal to Angel, who is captured and tortured by a vicious general named Mapache (Emilio Fernandez, who was born in 1904 and himself took part in the Revolution). The Bunch bravely attempt to rescue Angel, and are killed in the orgiastic final massacre, ending their days via the drama and violence they've cherished and lived by, rather than as imprisoned robbers or retired cowboys. The two surviving American characters decide to join up with the revolutionaries, whether for motives of idealism or excitement.

In 1965, two internationally-famous Frenchwomen, Jeanne Moreau and Brigitte Bardot, found

189

themselves cinematically involved in the Mexican Revolution in VIVA MARIA!, directed by Louis Malle. The noted French director told *Todo*, "Because of our own Revolution of 1789, we are more sympathetic to the Mexican Revolution than is Hollywood." However, European and American filmmakers both preferred to "visit" the Revolution and view it through their own characters' eyes, rather than the Mexicans'.

On the gentler side of things, 1969 also saw the release of POPI, starring Alan Arkin as a Puerto Rican widower working three jobs in Spanish Harlem, where he struggles to free his two young sons from the discouragements of ghetto life. Co-starring Miguel Alejandro and Ruben Figueroa, and Rita Moreno as Lupe, the film earned good reviews and was by turns touching and satirical. Arkin's performance was described as Chaplin-esque, and POPI includes classical slapstick sequences. "Hilarious! Brings the spirit of the Marx Brothers and Molly Goldberg to Spanish America," said *Newsweek*.

But commercially, the movie went nowhere, unlike its more violent and negative counterparts. (In 1976, POPI did make it to TV as a short-lived

(*Here, and on facing page*) Scenes from Sam Peckinpah's controversial THE WILD BUNCH (1969), starring William Holden and set during the Mexican Revolution

series starring Hector Elizondo.) Pedro Armendariz, who died in 1963, had told *Todo* magazine, "Whether here or in the USA, the public is underrated. They want a good story. If there's also sex or violence, so be it. But it has to fit the context.

"It's up to writers to create good stories, for studios want them. But if the stories are weak, they throw in sex and violence, as an audience lure."

How then to explain the failure of POPI, with its strong, uplifting storyline and laudable performances (on video, the film has become a cult favorite)? Alan Arkin informed the press, "We had a good product, but the studio didn't promote it. They knew it was good, and liked the reviews, but they figured nobody would go see a movie about a man and his sons." The joys and sorrows of a

Paul Newman, Mexican-style, and Claire Bloom in THE OUTRAGE (1964)

Ava Gardner, Richard Burton and Mexican working boys in
THE NIGHT OF THE IGUANA (1964)

single parent and his brood would seem to be a universal theme—unless Hollywood chose to view POPI strictly as the story of a *Puerto Rican* and his sons . . .

Fernando Lamas once said on TV, "Now and then a few good pictures get made, thanks to a persistent and well-connected producer or director. But oddly enough, it's the good pictures Hollywood is most afraid of." And often doesn't know how, or care, to market properly.

Anthony Quinn in THE 25TH HOUR (1967)

Yul Brynner in VILLA RIDES (1968)

Yul Brynner aids a Mexican woman in RETURN OF THE SEVEN (1966)

193

Pina Pellicer and Marlon Brando in ONE-EYED JACKS (1960)

Rita Moreno and Marlon Brando in THE
NIGHT OF THE FOLLOWING DAY (1968)

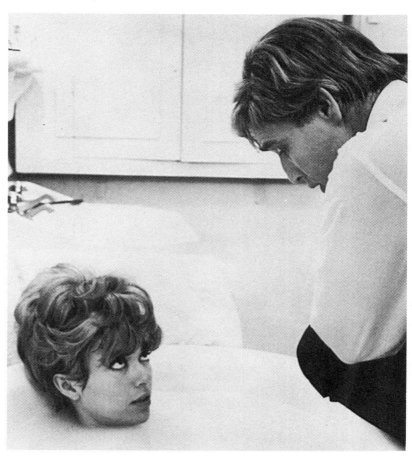

Linda Ronstadt, American-style

6. THE SEVENTIES:
Ethnic!

"I grew up in a New York neighborhood surrounded by seven or eight cultures—Puerto
Rican, Jewish, Italian, Irish, you name it. All this
soaked in like a sponge. For me, ethnic was
wonderful; I'm known as 'the man of a thou-
sand races'!"
                    —Hector Elizondo in *USA Today*, 1986

Like the bigger screen, TV's record when it came
to Hispanic characters was neither encouraging nor
equitable—excepting perhaps Duncan Renaldo's
Cisco Kid. Such characters, when they existed,
were minor or stereotypical, or both. Walter Brennan's hit series "The Real McCoys" featured an
ever-grinning, overly-obliging farmhand named
Pepino (meaning "cucumber"). Throughout the
show's run, Brennan repeatedly mispronounced it
Pepina, the feminine form of Pepino. This, despite
hundreds of reported letters urging a correct pro-
nunciation.

Another distinctly secondary character, on the
Western series "Rawhide," was named Jesus, a common first name in Spanish. But so as not to offend
any non-Hispanic viewers, his name in the credits
was phonetically spelled "Hey Soos"!

Major Hispanic stars like Dolores Del Rio and
Cesar Romero had guest-starred in prominent TV
roles as early as the 1950s. But again, they invariably
played remarkable, often nationality-less characters
far removed from the realities of most Hispanic or
for that matter non-Hispanic viewers. Fernando
Lamas was quoted in *Picture Screen*, "Television is

Warren Oates and Isela Vega in BRING ME THE HEAD OF ALFREDO GARCIA (1974)

like movies—in Hollywood, when they like you, they think of you as European, and cast you as a count or a duke. Is nice."

The small screen carried on the tradition of preferential casting of non-Hispanic performers in Hispanic parts, with the result that a few such actors, incarnating the few TV Latinos, represented "the invisible minority" to Middle America. Renaldo and Desi Arnaz were the main exceptions.

The most popular Hispanic TV character of the 1960s, at least among general audiences, was José Jimenez. The heavily accented, strangely ingratiating New York City hotel bellhop was the creation of Bill Dana, a writer/actor of Hungarian heritage (he was born William Szathmary). He launched Jimenez on Steve Allen's show in the late 1950s, then played him on Danny Thomas' comedy series, and finally starred as him in "The Bill Dana Show" from 1963-65. Dana's most famous line, "My name José Jimenez" (sic), quickly became a national catch-phrase.

Dana also appeared as Jimenez in nightclubs and on record albums. José, he declared, "is the nice side of everybody." In 1964, a Kalamazoo Girl Scout troop cited Jimenez for being "a chaste, honorable and amusing character."

But through the '60s, pressure from Hispanic groups was mounting. It focused on José as yet another dim-witted, English-mangling figure of fun, and on the fact that said fun was at Hispanics' expense and benefited a non-Hispanic. The inevitable winds of change signaled his demise, and on April 4, 1970, at a meeting of the Congress of Mexican-American Unity, Bill Dana announced, "After tonight, José Jimenez is dead." And at least for the '70s, he was, although on rare occasions subsequently, Dana has been encouraged to have José make a brief appearance.

Hispanic-American groups were able to exert a gradually effective pressure on the small screen. Therefore, by the end of the 1970s, two popular TV commercials stereotypes were permanently retired after sustained complaints and boycotts: the Frito Bandito, based on the cinematic greaser, and Chi-

Warren Oates and ruffians in BRING ME THE HEAD OF ALFREDO GARCIA

quita Banana, loosely based on Carmen Miranda. And beginning in the '70s, the manufacturers of Rosarita foods were very careful that their trademark character come across like a Hispanic Betty Crocker and not a culinary Lupe Velez.

By the late '60s and early '70s, the foundation had been laid for positive Hispanic TV characters and the birth of Hispanic TV stars. In 1967, "High Chaparral" debuted, and made highly visible stars, for a while, of Henry Darrow and Linda Cristal. Darrow, who had no accent, was allowed to essay a gamut of roles on TV, and attempted to break into movies. Cristal's role was atypical in that she played a strong and powerful *Hispana*. In 1982, 11 years after the series ended, she told this writer, "I was very conscious of being a role model. I received countless letters from the Spanish-speaking fans, thanking me, from at least 16 nations."

Linda later co-starred on the big screen with Charles Bronson, but her accent (and gender, as Hollywood grew more and more sexist in casting) kept her mostly on the sidelines. "I can only dream of a career like my idol's—Bette Davis—playing all ages and nationalities . . ."

A complete contrast to the serene, almost glacial

Ricardo Montalban, aka FANTASY ISLAND's Mr. Roarke

Late-1970s newcomer to Hollywood Edward James Olmos

and the Man." Prinze was a self-described "Hungar-ican," half Jewish Hungarian, half Puerto Rican. The series made him an overnight star and sex symbol, and his future looked bright indeed, but at 22 he killed himself (accidentally?) with a gun. More than one journalist dubiously asserted that fame and fortune had been too much for this "confused" young product of the *barrio*. (Playing Prinze in a later TV movie biography was then up-and-coming Ira Angustain, one of the high schoolers in the '70s series "The White Shadow." Angustain's star seemed to have faded after the film.)

The same year, 1977, saw the rise of another Puerto Rican TV star, Erik (Enrique) Estrada, who played one of two California Highway Patrol officers on "CHiPS", which lasted until 1983. TV stardom is of course exceedingly difficult to maintain

Fess Parker and Katy Jurado in SMOKY (1972)

Cristal was the hot-blooded, hyper Charo, the Spanish "coochie-coochie girl" and endless talk show guest of the '70s. Hailing from the province of Murcia, she parlayed the malapropisms and accent of a "looney Latina" into TV and Las Vegas stardom; her flaky image notwithstanding, she is an accomplished classical guitarist. Comedian Liz Torres made her mark on "Phyllis," a spin-off from "The Mary Tyler Moore Show," later moving into comic guest-starring roles on TV, one of the few *Hispanas* working in comedy—most recently as the "house Hispanic" on the Valerie Harper series "City."

In 1974, newcomer Freddie Prinze and veteran Jack Albertson co-starred in the hit sitcom "Chico

Screen siren Barbara Carrera

Actresses like Principal and Carter, and then Catherine Bach of "The Dukes of Hazzard," were unknown to the general public as part-Hispanic until their appearances as presenters or recipients on the nationally televised Golden Eagle Awards show devised by the pro-Hispanic Hollywood organization NOSOTROS.

NOSOTROS' distinguished founder Ricardo Montalban attained international TV stardom in the long-running (1978-84) "Fantasy Island," as the ageless, mysterious and ethnically vague Mr. Roarke. Earlier in the decade, Montalban appeared in a lively mix of TV movies, made-in-Hollywood PLANET OF THE APES sequels, and foreign features like the Italian LA SPINA DORSALE DEL DIAVOLO (1970; it meant The Devil's Backbone, but was released in the U.S. and U.K. as THE DESERTER).

Raquel Welch in KANSAS CITY BOMBER (1972)

beyond a given series, and Estrada did become a bigger celebrity than his Anglo counterpart Larry Wilcox. But by the late '80s he was relatively inactive, and usually got into the news, when he did, because of his private life. This may be due to his having become, like Prinze, a national heart-throb. Said Prinze, "If you're Hispanic, man, they think you really *got* something—downstairs."

"Dallas" bowed in 1978, and made an international TV star of former film actress-turned-agent Victoria Principal. There were however recurring complaints that the series, set in Texas, had no Hispanic-American characters. (In the mid-'80s, when Nicaraguan Barbara Carrera came aboard for a season, she played a Euro-type tycoon-temptress, not a typical Centroamericana.) Another '70s TV star partly of Latin origin was Lynda "Wonder Woman" Carter, who later portrayed Rita Hayworth in a TV film.

Music, like TV and unlike motion pictures, made a number of Hispanic stars—though some very temporary—during this time. TV shot the personable singer Trini Lopez to stardom in the early '60s, and spurred the popularity of Vikki Carr (neé Florencia Bisenta de Casillas Martinez Cardona). In 1967, Carr was Grammy-nominated for her hit

Richard Burton and
Raquel Welch in BLUE-
BEARD (1972)

Perry King and Raquel Welch in THE WILD PARTY (1974)

Maria Felix, Anthony Quinn and Dolores Del Rio at party celebrating THE CHILDREN OF SANCHEZ (1978)

"It Must Be Him," and in 1972 recorded the first in a string of successful Spanish-language albums. Hers was a rare case of a performer's Spanish market catching up with, then surpassing, her English market sales.

Singer Eydie Gorme has proclaimed her heritage as a Sephardic Jew (that is, of Spanish or Portuguese origin). In her teens, she worked in Spanish-language radio in New York, and later duplicated her popularity in the United States gaining international fame in Mexico and beyond, recording hit albums in Spanish with Trio Los Panchos.

Also of Spanish origin, Joan Baez was "the queen of folk" throughout the '60s and '70s, eventually becoming as well known for her pro-peace activism and bisexual stance as for her music. Like Vikki Carr, Linda Ronstadt has had a lasting career, and a varied one. Her image has alternated between rock, pop, even country, and in the early '80s she tried operetta in a film of THE PIRATES OF PENZANCE (which she also had done on Broadway). But she seemed less at home in petticoats than—at decade's end—in her *charra* outfit, raising her voice to her Hispanic forebears in the album, concert tours and TV special "Canciones De Mi Padre" (Songs of My Father).

More notably Hispanic singers included Tony Orlando, at the time still with Dawn, his two-woman backup group, and José Feliciano, sometimes labeled the Puerto Rican Stevie Wonder. (Orlando occasionally undertakes an acting assignment, but was totally miscast playing Jose Ferrer in the television movie biography of Rosemary Clooney.) Also Freddie Fender, who helped revive "Mexican country" (labled Tex-Mex) with favorites like "Wasted Days and Wasted Nights," "Alla en el Rancho Grande" (which had made a star of Tito Guizar) and "Vaya Con Dios." Meanwhile, in Spain and elsewhere, Julio Iglesias was building his record-breaking reputation, though it would be well into the '80s before he cracked the U.S. market as a latter day matinee idol.

On the classical front, Placido Domingo and Julia Migenes—whom some consider the best

(*Here, and on facing page*) Five faces
of Hector Elizondo

From symphonic to disco music, the 1970s proved that music and *Hispanidad* go together like salt and tequila. Dancer-actress Margo, who was Xavier Cugat's niece (Charo was at one point his wife), opined, "Ethnic is 'in,' now! The '70s are rediscovering the Latin sound and sending it out to everybody, just as in the 1940s. The one thing we are missing is those wonderful '40s musicals."

While music and television were forming or solidifying several celebrity careers, Hollywood's Hispanic film stars were generally doing better in the '70s than during the lean '60s. If they worked

operatic Carmen since Callas—were injecting opera with new vigor, and composer-conductor Lalo Schifrin was creating TV themes like "Mission: Impossible" and "Starsky and Hutch," as well as film scores for COOL HAND LUKE and others. On the rock end of the spectrum, Jerry Garcia's The Grateful Dead and the Chicano *raza*-rock band Los Lobos enjoyed global success. The Hispanic contribution to American and international music ranged far beyond salsa, tango or Iglesias.

Nor were all such efforts predictable. In the late '60s, singing housewife Mrs. Miller's off-key, falsetto renditions of contemporary hits like "Downtown" made her an overnight fad. And in the late '70s, when Hollywood finally decided to mount an expensive film bio of the century's greatest male ballet dancer, NIJINSKY was played not by the obvious, if somewhat aged, choices of Nureyev or Baryshnikov, but by Argentine ballet star George (Jorje) de la Peña.

Anthony Quinn

Anthony Quinn in MOHAMMAD: MESSENGER OF GOD (1976)

less often, it was mostly through choice, for, following the loud consciousness-raising of the late '60s, the '70s discovered and rejoiced in America's ethnicity. Of course in Hollywood that usually translated to Italian or Jewish. The decade saw a shift to recognizably ethnic characters no longer trying to drown their difference in a melting pot, and such characters made superstars of Barbra Streisand, Dustin Hoffman, Robert De Niro, Al Pacino, Sylvester Stallone, etc.

"Blaxploitation" films also flourished, and Slavic characters—especially Polish ones—were not ignored. But the sincere exploration of American subcultures seemed limited to those with an English-language base. Thus, unaccented stars like Rita Moreno and Cesar Romero seldom got the chance to depict on screen any of the varieties of the Hispanic-American experience. Following the failure of POPI, Moreno gave a tour-de-force cameo performance in the landmark CARNAL KNOWLEDGE

Irene Dailey, Jack Albertson and newcomer Martin Sheen recording the original Broadway cast album of THE SUBJECT WAS ROSES (1967)

Martin Sheen

(1971), did assorted movies, toured in a lucrative nightclub act, and played the recurring role of a Slavic hooker on "The Rockford Files" on TV, earning upwards of $50,000 an episode and an Emmy award.

In 1979, she appeared in HAPPY BIRTHDAY, GEMINI, from Albert Innaurato's play about Italian-Americans; her sole noteworthy film role in the '80s was a voluble Italian-American wife in Alan Alda's hit comedy THE FOUR SEASONS. Moreno's one juicy Puerto Rican role of the '70s was chanteuse Googie Gomez in THE RITZ (1976), recreating her Tony-winning performance from Terence McNally's hit Broadway play set in a gay Manhattan bathhouse.

"Googie," she explained, "is a singer with absolutely no talent whatever, but all the ambition and chutzpah in the world. She actually believes she would be as big a star as Streisand today, if she'd just gotten the same breaks." On video and in revivals, THE RITZ has become a camp cult classic, and Moreno often reprises the super-accented Googie in her act and on TV. Says Googie, "I wass a nun in the oreeginal cast of THE SOUND OF MUSIC. Een fact, I wass more oreeginal than anyone!"

Cesar Romero, who professed never to take him-

Oscar-winning Cuban cinematographer Nestor Almendros (SOPHIE'S CHOICE, KRAMER VS. KRAMER, THE BLUE LAGOON, PLACES IN THE HEART)

Gilbert Roland, age 70

Gilbert Roland and Beau Bridges in THE CHRISTIAN LICORICE STORE (1971)

self too seriously, began the decade in THE COMPUTER WORE TENNIS SHOES and ended it with MONSTER. He continued to do television, and became famous for looking-great-for-his-age and for being an inveterate Hollywood partygoer. "Charming Cesar would attend the opening of a napkin," wrote one local columnist.

Rita Hayworth often complained that Hollywood never took her very seriously, and its neglect became glaringly apparent as she aged, even though beautifully. Her films, usually independents, went from bad to worse, sometimes set in Hispanic locales, as in the 1970 ROAD TO SALINA and two years later her last major role, in THE WRATH OF GOD, set in Mexico during the Revolution. Hayworth reasoned, "There's no point to making movies if they don't hold anyone's interest. After all, it is hard work, and you want it to mean something."

Raquel Welch opened the '70s as an ex-male (played by Rex Reed) in the highly-publicized flop MYRA BRECKINRIDGE, and played increasingly liberated women, then went to Europe to make BLUEBEARD (1972), THE THREE MUSKETEERS (1973) and L'ANIMAL (1977). Having proven her deftness at

Gilbert Roland in THE BLACK PEARL (1977)

comedy, she finished the decade with a spectacular performance as a Native American who ages from young squaw to ancient crone in the TV movie THE LEGEND OF WALKS FAR WOMAN.

Katy Jurado chose to work less frequently, on

TV, in France, and in the features PAT GARRETT AND BILLY THE KID (1973) and the Mexican film THE CHILDREN OF SANCHEZ (1978), which starred Anthony Quinn as a struggling barrio paterfamilias. SANCHEZ also starred Dolores Del Rio in her final film, her only one in the '70s. She later stated, "It was a pleasure to act, but with time I came to feel my charity work was more important . . . I was happy enough to view the films of my peers like Cantinflas and Maria Felix, with everyone else."

Carlos Montalban and Woody Allen in BANANAS (1971)

Howard Cosell interviews BANANAS' General Vargas (Carlos Montalban)

Woody Allen dallies with Natividad Abascal in BANANAS

Ruben Blades (left) with Sam Elliott and Whoopi Goldberg in FATAL BEAUTY (1987)

Ruben Blades and Jack Nicholson in THE TWO JAKES (1990)

Julio Iglesias with TV host Luca Bentivoglio

Linda Ronstadt, Mexican-style

Trini Lopez

Gilbert Roland worked mostly abroad, in French and Italian productions, then appeared in GAUGUIN, THE SAVAGE (1979). As always, he preferred to embody men of action. Likewise Fernando Lamas, who when not behind the cameras directing, alternated between action flicks and suave roles, as in THE CHEAP DETECTIVE (1978).

And of course new celebrities came along, including Hollywood and New York's first famous Nicaraguan women. The latter, Bianca Jagger, gained fame via marriage to androgynous "look-alike" Mick Jagger, then via the Andy Warhol/Studio 54 Manhattan nightclubbing scene. Eventually Jagger tried her hand at acting, in a few pictures, most of them European-financed and none of them widely seen in the U.S.

Barbara Carrera went from modeling to movies via THE MASTER GUNFIGHTER (1975), in which she played a sedate señorita—mantilla and all—in the Old West. She was prematurely crowned "the new Dolores Del Rio," then did an about-face as the demonic title character in EMBRYO (1976), a Rock

Placido Domingo

Hudson starrer. She vamped her way through films like THE ISLAND OF DR. MOREAU (1977) and the James Bond-er NEVER SAY NEVER AGAIN (1983), and on TV's "Dallas." Her best roles were on TV as the Hawaiian EMMA, QUEEN OF THE SOUTH SEAS, as an ancient-day Israelite in MASADA, and a Native American in CENTENNIAL.

Martin Sheen (né Ramon Estevez in 1940) is lately known as the founder of an acting dynasty that includes sons Emilio Estevez and Charlie Sheen—he has another son and a daughter in the business—and as an activist against nuclear energy and for peace in Central America. He's also a widely-heralded actor whose career highpoint was probably Francis Coppola's 1979 Vietnam epic APOCALYPSE NOW. Sheen stole the film from Brando and Robert Duvall, giving such a strenuous performance that he suffered a heart attack while

Vikki Carr

doing it. Nor has Sheen ever been Oscar-nominated . . .

Sheen had a longstanding ambition someday to play his two political heroes, John F. Kennedy and Robert F. Kennedy, which he accomplished on TV, and well.

His film debut was in THE INCIDENT (1967). The following year he participated in the prestigious THE SUBJECT WAS ROSES (repeating his stage role), then made several acclaimed and trendsetting telefilms in the 1970s, including the first with a gay theme, THAT CERTAIN SUMMER, in 1972, plus THE EXECUTION OF PRIVATE SLOVIK and THE MISSILES OF OCTOBER—as Robert Kennedy during the Bay of Pigs debacle. Subsequent features cast him opposite Sophia Loren, Jodie Foster, etc., but other than the classic BADLANDS (1974), motion pictures largely wasted his talent until APOCALYPSE NOW. In 1988's WALL STREET, he played son Charlie Sheen's blue-collar father but took no billing.

1971 marked the screen debut of Mexican-Irish Sheen's friend and sometime co-star Hector Elizondo (born 1936), Puerto Rican on his mother's side, Basque on his father's. His bow was the Burt Lancaster vehicle VALDEZ IS COMING (described later), but in the 1960s he'd made a considerable

Alan Bates and George de la Peña in NIJINSKY (1979)

impact off-Broadway as a Puerto Rican locker room attendant in STEAMBATH, which won him an Obie award. Unlike Sheen, Elizondo—a talented "ethnic chameleon"—didn't change his name, and had trouble establishing himself in Hollywood, despite his theatrical training:

"I'll be damned if they call me a Latin actor. Nobody calls Sinatra an Italian singer. I'm an actor, period . . . I've gotten all these roles on my own. Just think how many I would have gotten if my name was not Elizondo." Still, the Buddhist actor has played everything from an undertaker to an assistant district attorney (shades of Burt Lancaster!), a plumber, a boxer, a Portuguese garbage barge captain, and a Cuban army captain—with and without toupee, creating even more versatility.

His films include THE TAKING OF PELHAM 1-2-3 (1974), CUBA (1978), and such '80s hits as YOUNG DOCTORS IN LOVE, THE FLAMINGO KID and NOTH-ING IN COMMON. He's also starred in three TV series based on movies—"Popi," "Freebie and the

Tony Orlando

215

"Queen of folk" Joan Baez

Bean" (as, you guessed it, "the Bean") and "Down and Out in Beverly Hills." In the first two, ironically, he took the roles created by Alan Arkin.

In 1980, *Talk* critic Wyatt Cooper wrote, "The '70s have seen a preponderance of films that failed to probe beneath the trendy surface, and a shunting of certain basic movie genres to the far rear . . . 'Ethnic' movies have selected picturesque stereotypes over the conflicting pressures of cultivating one's heritage in a nation founded on assimilation . . . Women's films, social problem films of the kind Warners did so well in its heyday, and historical pictures have all been put into deep hibernation."

More and more, Hollywood was targeting a thrill-seeking younger audience, and relying on easy formulas, particularly souped-up chases and ever more explicit violence. In the early 1970s, Westerns were still very popular, but quite formulaic. Whether made in the U.S., Spain, Mexico or Italy, a great percentage of them now included Mexico (but never south of Mexico) in their itineraries. Subtle stories like MY DARLING CLEMENTINE and HIGH NOON, where one, two or even a handful of men die during the climax—without gushing blood—were a thing of the past. Filmmakers were now trying for climaxes from the word "go."

THE FIVE MAN ARMY (1970), for instance, was a self-proclaimed "action tale" set in 1914 Mexico, filmed in Spain and Italy, and top-lining TV actor Peter Graves (of "Mission: Impossible"). ARMY borrowed inspiration from THE PROFESSIONALS, with its team of destructive experts, e.g., one in dynamite, one proficient at firearms, and a Japanese (Tetsuro Tamba) adept at slicing torsos in half. This team is rounded up by a Mexican revolutionary (Italian Nino Castelnuovo) to steal a $500,000 shipment of gold being delivered by rail to a despotic general.

Bob Hope was reprimanded by the Mexican government for this TV skit in which Lee Marvin played Slim Premise, Johnine Lee played Chiquita and he played "Mexican bandit" El Crummo

216

The gang plans to capture the gold, subtract a hefty commission, and pass the balance on to local revolutionaries. One gold-hungry professional explains, "Some men die for money, and some die for causes." The lead characters in these Westerns, of course, die for the former.

EL CONDOR (1970) was a made-in-Spain Western starring Lee Van Cleef and black ex-football star Jim Brown as two soldiers of fortune who hire an Apache tribe headed by Chief Santana (Iron Eyes Cody) to help them storm a fortress in Mexico named El Condor which houses a treasure of gold. CANNON FOR CORDOBA (1970), its name redolent of GUNS FOR SAN SEBASTIAN, was another high-charged saga of bandits and revolutionaries, this time in 1912 Mexico. It starred George Peppard, Raf Vallone and a mostly Italian supporting cast.

"Spaghetti Western" director Damiano Damiani admitted, "We cast our own people as Mexicans. We have no Mexicans in Europe. But what excuse does Hollywood have?"

As screen morality became open to interpretation, bandits were no longer automatically the bad guys; it was now less a matter of who was doing what, but *why*. On the up side, Mexican revolutionaries were generally depicted as good guys, even if occasionally corrupt—a far cry from the standard policy of silents and early talkies.

The British-Spanish production A TOWN CALLED HELL (1971) bucked the trend by setting its violence—featuring Telly Savalas, Stella Stevens and Robert Shaw—in late 19th century Mexico. Shaw, who'd played Henry VIII in the Oscar-winning A MAN FOR ALL SEASONS, told British *Photoplay*, "I'm doing this for money . . . I play a priest, which is not exactly typecasting . . . The movie's full of violence, and you learn next to nothing about Mexico, but why else would anyone agree to do something like A TOWN CALLED BASTARD (its U.K. title) except for money?"

1971 saw the release—but not widely, in the U.S.—of the plainly named PANCHO VILLA, starring Western actor Clint Walker. Italy's *Oggi* magazine declared, "There is little to distinguish this from other brawling spectacles set in Old Mexico. Nor is it a bio of the infamous revolutionary, but more an excuse to cash in on Villa's celluloid charisma by patterning the film's chief bandit after Villa." Sort of plagiarizing history.

VALDEZ IS COMING (1971) stood head and shoul-

Martin Sheen in BADLANDS (1974)

ders above the preceding titles, only partly because of Burt Lancaster's textured performance. He played Valdez, a Mexican-American peace officer and former cavalry scout—"I used to chase Indians before I knew better." Racism is again spotlighted in this Lancaster film, where due to the machinations of a corrupt cattle baron (Jon Cypher), Valdez accidentally kills a black man suspected of a murder he did not commit.

When Valdez tries to collect money for the man's pregnant Native American widow, he is tortured by the cattle baron's thugs. After being shot in the ear and semi-crucified in the roasting desert, Valdez deposits the squaw with his friend Diego (Frank Silvera) and informs Cypher's henchman, "Valdez is coming." Armed with his Sharps army rifle, a shotgun and a pistol, Valdez confronts the cattleman at his hacienda and demands $100 for the Indian woman. Surrounded by henchmen, Valdez shoots his way out and takes with him Cypher's woman

217

(Susan Clark), whom he holds hostage in return for the $100 contribution.

The villain's men pursue Valdez, who kills off five of them and ignites the love of Ms. Clark. The requisite showdown pits Valdez against the remaining henchmen, whose admiring leader El Segundo (Barton Heyman) orders to go home and leave Valdez alone with the beef baron. But the coward refuses to draw, afraid of Valdez's sharp-shooting skill. "I should have killed you three days ago," he scowls. Valdez retorts, "Or paid the $100." So ends the private war of Bob Valdez.

The New York Times enthused, "Mr. Lancaster is simply beyond criticism, an enduring star whose screen personality—decent, liberal, tough, well-intentioned—provides the shape of the movies that are constructed around him." For a change, Lancaster played an underdog, yet came up a winner.

Another star vehicle was the 1971 comedy BANANAS, directed and co-written by Woody Allen. He played the hapless Fielding Mellish, who finds himself stuck in the dangerous Latin land of "San Marcos," where he winds up impersonating Castro. But Mellish is merely a Groucho Marxist, and though the film contains every imaginable banana republic stereotype, this is offset by antic comedy which pokes fun at everyone, including urban New Yorkers, middle-Americans, and Mellish himself.

"With its hijinks that embrace crazy dictators, torturers, CIA operatives and passionate señoritas, BANANAS would be unbelievable or offensive were it not so grounded in the ludicrous truth," said critic Wyatt Cooper. "Its steady flow of jokes, sight-gags and parody make it one of the funniest pictures within memory."

Back in the humorless mode, the underrated DUCK, YOU SUCKER (1972), also known as A FISTFUL OF DYNAMITE, was originally titled ONCE UPON A TIME, THE REVOLUTION—this time out, 1913. Rod Steiger, if you can believe it, plays a peasant named Juan Miranda who turns—of course—to banditry. The co-star is James Coburn as an Irish dynamite expert and IRA supporter who desires to involve Miranda in the Revolution. (It's not explained what the Irishman is doing in Mexico, or why his mission is converting Miranda.)

SUCKER suffers from a loophole script and the heavy-handed touch of director Sergio Leone, whose Western/Revolution films were less political and more blatantly commercial than other Italian directors' and many Americans.' Juan demurs, "I don't want to be a hero. I want the money." The zealot Irishman converts to Juan's cynicism after somehow finding that the Revolution isn't what he'd believed it to be, and tosses away his ideals along with his Revolutionary textbook.

THE WRATH OF GOD (1972) featured another Irish terrorist on the lam in Mexico, but during the late 1920s, therefore surrounded by a greater number of machine-guns, one of them brandished by defrocked priest Robert Mitchum. WRATH's chief villain is Frank Langella, whose devoutly religious mother Señora de la Plata—Rita Hayworth, no less—finally guns him down! The plot is murky and the violence nonstop. Kevin Thomas of the *Los Angeles Times* called it "a hypocritical, brutalizing cartoon of a film that makes fun of the violence it ostensibly deplores. (But) it becomes a demoralizing experience."

The Hollywood Reporter wondered, "Shouldn't it have been helmed by Sam Peckinpah?" (Ralph Nelson directed it.) Thomas added, "Thankfully, Rita Hayworth, elegant and beautiful, fares pretty well. It is unfortunate she is not on-screen more often because she lends WRATH a note of dignity it so desperately needs." Sadly, Hayworth's first Latina role in decades was her last.

THE REVENGERS, also 1972, included Susan Hayward's last movie performance. Once more, the leading lady was under-utilized in a secondary role, at a time when Hollywood seemed to have forgotten that women could co-star in, or even carry, a motion picture. The violence-drenched story centers on William Holden, whose family has been killed by a gang of Indians led by two white men. The law will do nothing, and the culprits have fled into Mexico, so Holden follows them, and south of the border takes the law into his own hands.

Holden recruits six convicts, experts in violence—à la THE PROFESSIONALS—including sadistic Ernest Borgnine and black actor Woody Strode, and the seven (an important number, after THE MAGNIFICENT SEVEN's success) target the two whites, and kill one of them. Holden is wounded, then nursed back to health and humanity by potato-growing Irish nurse Susan Hayward, who tells him, "You live in your heart, and you've got to be careful what you put in your heart." Holden agrees that he wants no "worms" (revenge) in his heart, and gives up his half-completed vengeance.

In THE DEADLY TRACKERS (1973), Richard Harris is the Cooperesque sheriff of "Santa Rosa." He has never shot anyone, and eschews a gun. Revenge enters his heart when Rod Taylor's gang of bank robbers murders his wife and son. This gang is exceptionally violent—one member gleefully recounts how he killed his father, and another sports, in place of an amputated hand, a chunk of railroad tie which he uses to smash open watermelons and heads. The gang also has terrible table manners—they never use silverware—and a habit of heading for Mexico after each crime.

Harris pursues Taylor and company down south, where he is aided by his Mexican counterpart (Al Lettieri). The Mexican wishes to see justice done, to bring the gang in alive and have them tried. Harris, however, simply wants them butchered, and together or separately, he and Lettieri pursue the wild bunch, with buckets of blood en route. "Out-Peckinpahs Peckinpah," said *Variety*, also condemning the overstated ending in which the moral is delivered with one final blast of a gun.

All too often, Mexico and Hispanics were still synonymous with violence. Critic Vincent Canby pointed out that in the 1973 Robert Duvall action movie, BADGE 373, about street gangs, Puerto Ricans are blamed for every evil deed that occurs in the story. The Puerto Rican Action Coalition asked Paramount's president Frank Yablans to withdraw the "racist" movie from exhibition, but he refused. Both THE WARRIORS (1978) and BOULEVARD NIGHTS (1979) extended the habit of linking Hispanics with violence, despite protests by Puerto Ricans, Chicanos and others.

Activist organizations had more success on TV, where the Hispanic gang member as villain became less frequent, and Freddie Prinze's depiction of the "shiftless" Chico was toned down, as were The Man's anti-Hispanic epithets. Thanks to Hispanic-American pressure, Hispanic employment on "Chico and the Man" was augmented. And in 1978 an episode of Ed Asner's "Lou Grant" which dealt with the problems of illegal aliens in Los Angeles was widely praised for its sensitivity and insight.

Even when it didn't focus on Hispanic themes, TV became a breeding ground for Hispanic character actors and stars, some of them moving on to fea-

Hollywood newcomer Martin Sheen

ture films. A sampling of such personalities includes soap opera hunk A Martinez, Rachel Ticotin (who co-starred with Paul Newman in FORT APACHE: THE BRONX), Jose Perez (of the series "On the Rocks" and "Calucci's Department"), Gregory Sierra (of TV's BARNEY MILLER), Richard Yniguez (who played Santa Anna in the telefilm HOUSTON, THE LEGEND OF TEXAS), Ned Romero (who alternates Hispanic and native American roles), and veteran character actress and acting coach Carmen Zapata.

Television films have presented a variety of Hispanic stories set here and abroad, i.e., EVITA PERON, starring Faye Dunaway, with Jose Ferrer as singer Augustin Magaldi, and also starring Katy Jurado, Rita Moreno and Pedro Armendariz Jr.; DEATH PENALTY, with Colleen Dewhurst as a psychologist rehabilitating members of a Hispanic-American street gang; and THE STREETS OF L.A.,

Anthony Quinn

starring Joanne Woodward, about Los Angeles gangs, and featuring a large Hispanic cast, among them Fernando Allende in his American debut and Isela Vega.

In 1974, in an article in *The New Yorker*, critic Pauline Kael asseverated that Westerns were dead. In 1976, there was a cluster of Westerns coinciding with the American Bicentennial—though, curiously, no films at the time were made about the American Revolution—but by the late '70s Westerns had mostly gone the way of those other hibernating genres that once peopled the screen.

In essence, this meant fewer Hispanic characterizations. Qualitatively, Hispanics' position wasn't affected or improved by any given (or taken away) genre. In ZANDY'S BRIDE (1974), Gene Hackman is a California frontiersman who buys a mail-order bride and returns her because she is Mexican. She is replaced by Liv Ullmann from Minneapolis, who will give him what the *mestiza* couldn't, white offspring.

MR. MAJESTYK (1974) posits two implausible Hispanics in the form of Charles Bronson as a Slavic-Mexican farm owner and Linda Cristal as his girlfriend Nancy Chavez. The picture brazenly advertised itself as a paean to migrant farm workers, but was a vehicle for Bronson-as-Superman. Vincent Majestyk (notice, he and the film weren't named, say, Mr. Martinez) hires Mexican immigrants to work his watermelon patch. Italian-American mobsters who preferred him to hire Americans retaliate by machine-gunning his stored melons. The infuriated Majestyk responds by destroying the mob single-handedly, then drives off into the sunset with the Chicana field worker whose jeans, in the words of one critic, "have remained spotless after weeks of working crops."

Sam Peckinpah's BRING ME THE HEAD OF ALFREDO GARCIA (1974) was a resounding and bizarre flop about a down-at-heels bar owner (Warren Oates) who wears a motorcycle jacket embroidered with "Viva Zapata" and spends most of his time speaking to a fly-infested head resting on the front seat of his old red convertible. The film includes a character named Fred C. Dobbs (Bogart's character in THE TREASURE OF THE SIERRA MADRE), but is no classic. It simple-mindedly pits "good" country Mexicans against "bad" city Mexicans, and displays Peckinpah's pessimism and blood-lust, along with contemporary elements like noisy airplanes, teeming slums and menacing gangsters.

Post-Westerns, Hispanic characters began showing up as lesser parts in varying genres, i.e., the WWII film MIDWAY (1976) included a Hispanic character nicknamed Chili Bean. His token minutes of screen time were due in part to the interminable all-star Anglo cast and battle scenes. In a similar vein, FREEBIE AND THE BEAN (1974) had provided Alan Arkin as the Bean with another ethnic outing, but was primarily a violent action vehicle for James Caan, instead of a "relevant" buddy movie.

Likewise, CUBA (1979) was little more than an exotic setting with hissable villains for the love affair between Sean Connery as a British mercenary and dark-haired Brooke Adams as a local aristocrat's wife in the Batista era.

In sum, the '70s didn't do that much for Hispanics on the silver screen, but they did make the once derided concept of ethnicity increasingly acceptable. With time, and because of Hispanics' growing numbers, that concept—that being different isn't better or worse, just a fact of life—trickled down, and eventually reached Hollywood.

Rita Hayworth in THE WRATH OF GOD (1972)

Raul Julia in ROMERO (1989)

7. THE EIGHTIES:
Strength in Numbers?

"All I ever wanted to be was myself."
　—Rita Hayworth in *Motion Picture*, 1975

The 1980s saw the passing of three Hispanic stars: Fernando Lamas, Dolores Del Rio and Rita Hayworth. Lamas died in 1982 in his mid sixties. A few years before his death, he told the press, "I have been very lucky. I always knew I had little talent. But I came along early enough so my type was still in vogue, and from my type, I made a career." The Latin Lover is today an outmoded figure. Once, only a "hot-blooded" male dared to show passion; today, unabashed carnality is expected from leading men whatever their national origin.

Dolores Del Rio died in 1983 in her late seventies. She too was under no delusions that she could have become a Hollywood star during just any decade. In 1979, she confessed, "Beauty was my top asset. Then acting, once I learned how . . . I arrived

during the silents, and became important enough so that in talkies my accent was overruled by my stardom and looks.

"I tried always to keep my looks." And she did, rivaled only by Dietrich in the ageless-glamour sweepstakes, supposedly never exposing her perfect complexion to the sun, and sleeping a reported 12 hours a day. By the time of her passing, even Hollywood had forgotten how big a star she had been.

In the early '30s, producer David O. Selznick informed his staff, "I want Dolores Del Rio in a South Seas romance . . . I don't care what story you use so long as we call it BIRD OF PARADISE and Del Rio jumps into a flaming volcano at the finish." And so, the star and Joel McCrea, director King Vidor

Raul Julia in THE MORNING AFTER (1986)

it's the accent that's more likely to impede stellar casting, but even that can be mitigated by talent like Raul Julia's.

Today's "Lat Pack" of up-and-coming stars may seem less exotic to mainstream audiences because, unlike most of yesteryear's stars, they're not Mexican, Cuban, Brazilian or Argentinian. They're Hispanic-Americans (sometimes *half* Hispanic-Americans) who look, sound and act like everyone else. Also gone is the glamorous aura which enveloped Del Rio and Lamas as form-fittingly as their accents. For the most part, today's Hispanic stars are interchangeable, casting-wise, with their down-to-earth Anglo, Italo or Scandinavian colleagues.

The deans of the newer set of Latino actors are Raul Julia and Edward James Olmos, exceptionally versatile and committed character actor/stars. The Puerto Rican Julia was born in 1944 and is almost as well-known for Shakespeare and other classical stage roles and musicals as for film. In 1971, he debuted in small parts in THE ORGANIZATION and PANIC IN NEEDLE PARK, finally coming into his own in Hollywood in the '80s. His roles fall into two cat-

and a Hollywood crew traveled to Polynesia and did just that.

Rita Hayworth died in 1987 in her late sixties. Unlike Lamas and Del Rio, she was an American star. Not because of her name change, but because she was born and raised here. Yet even without an accent in English, had she not been re-dubbed *Hayworth*, it's doubtful she'd have become a star of any magnitude, for she wouldn't have been picked for grooming by her studio.

Therein lies the major difference between yesterday's and today's Hispanic stars. Today they *can* be Hispanic—on- and off-screen—for all the world to see. Surnames like Alonso, Julia, Olmos, Peña and Zuñiga may (so far) inhibit the mass appeal required for true super-stardom, but varying degrees of stardom have already been attained by the likes of Maria Conchita, Raul, Edward James, Elizabeth and Daphne, to name a few. Nowadays

Raul Julia in FLORIDA STRAITS (1986)

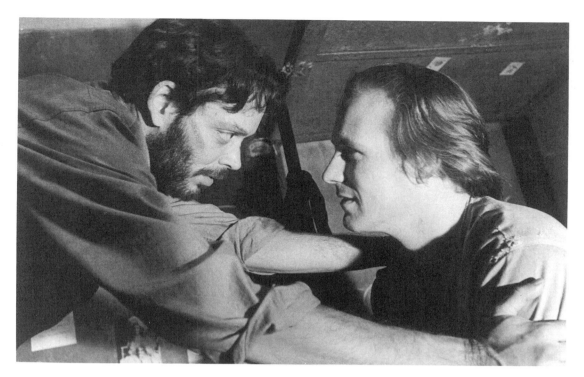

egories—support in big-budget star vehicles and lead roles in smaller-budgeted Latin-themed pictures.

In Jane Fonda's THE MORNING AFTER (1986), Julia played her hairdresser ex-husband, who loses her to Jeff Bridges and is revealed as the villain. In COMPROMISING POSITIONS (1985), he was David Suarez, a cop with whom the married heroine (Susan Sarandon in the movie) has an affair in the book. But not, for some reason, in the *movie* . . . Julia was wasted in the trite and stereotypical MOON OVER PARADOR (1988), as a blond South American VIP named Strausmann. The name recalls late Paraguayan dictator Alfredo Stroessner, and the film's title country is a merger of Paraguay and Ecuador. Brazilian Sonia Braga and Charo also lent their talents to the Richard Dreyfuss vehicle in which he impersonates the local dictator.

Julia co-starred in the acclaimed KISS OF THE SPIDER WOMAN (1985), from the novel by Argentine Manuel Puig. He played a Marxist sharing a jail cell with an apolitical gay man (William Hurt, who won the Academy Award for Best Actor). Brazilian Hector Babenco directed the story of how two men affect one another for the better—Hurt tempering Julia's rigidity and homophobia, and Julia raising Hurt's consciousness about the corrupt government under which they live and should struggle.

Raul Julia, Richard Dreyfuss and Sonia Braga in MOON OVER PARADOR (1988)

The roles were evenly matched, yet it was Hurt who stole the reviews and got an Oscar nomination. Spain's *Pantalla Dorada* (Golden Screen) dissented. "Hurt is a pallid American heterosexual enacting a South American with no trace of accent, and no quality of seeming Latin. His gay character is a stereotype, and no more a stretch for him than playing a Communist revolutionary is for Julia. After all, one

A Hispanized Richard Dreyfuss in MOON OVER PARADOR

LA GRAN FIESTA (*The Big Party*), the first full-length movie out of Puerto Rico, about a ball that becomes a political minefield when a conservative business-man schemes with foreign government officials to discredit the liberal governor. Marcos Zurinaga directed the Spanish-language picture.

Julia took center-stage in ROMERO (1989), about outspoken Salvadoran archbishop Oscar Romero, who was assassinated in 1980 during a church ser-vice. The independent film earned sizeable reviews, if not audiences, and featured Ana Alicia, Eddie Velez and Tony Perez. It was directed by Australian John Duignan, and taken to task by the Los Angeles *Reader* for "allowing American actors playing Sal-vadorans to say their lines in accented English." The paper added, "It's a pity more people will recall the fiery Julia from his roles in ONE FROM THE HEART, THE EYES OF LAURA MARS and TEQUILA SUNRISE than in this stirring movie."

Sonia Braga and Richard Dreyfuss: *tango*! in PARADOR

meets far more gay men in the movie business than guerrillas . . ."

On television, Julia played not only a flamboyant Santa Anna in 13 DAYS AT THE ALAMO but also a physically unlikely Onassis (with Anthony Quinn as his father) in ONASSIS—THE RICHEST MAN IN THE WORLD.

In 1986, Julia co-starred with E.G. Marshall in

Edward James Olmos (born 1947) bowed in Robert Young's independent film ALAMBRISTA!, about a young man's arduous and disappointing journey from Mexico to the U.S. "to make some money." Olmos played a wino looking for night-work, and another cameo was filled by Miguel Piñero, who wrote the play SHORT EYES. ALAM-BRISTA! was a rare and unsensationalized look at

Fernando Rey and Charo in MOON OVER PARADOR

Eddie Velez and Raul Julia in ROMERO

the plight of illegal immigrants. It won the Golden Camera prize at Cannes in 1977, and was unique in using English only when its protagonist encounters English-speaking characters, thus lending a sense of the newcomer's discomfort and disorientation.

Olmos attracted Hollywood's attention as El Pachuco in the 1979 play ZOOT SUIT by Luis Valdez, in Los Angeles. Two years later he recreated his acclaimed role as a combination legend, folk hero and guardian angel in the film version, which was shot by Universal in 11 days for only $2.5 million. Valdez wrote the screenplay and directed the story based on L.A.'s Sleepy Lagoon murder mystery of 1942, in which several Chicanos were railroaded into life sentences on a faked murder charge. That year also witnessed race riots in which flamboyantly zoot-suited Latinos were beaten or murdered by local ruffians and soldiers on leave from the war. The violence occurred with the tacit neutrality and in some cases participation of the local police.

Daniel Valdez starred as the young Chicano unknowingly headed for trouble, with Olmos as his zoot-suited alter ego. The murder trial scenes were explosive, and the fine supporting cast included Rose Portillo, Tyne Daly and Mike Gomez.

ZOOT SUIT, like ALAMBRISTA!, yielded further "proof" that Hispanic-themed movies languish at the box office. Despite personal raves, Olmos was cast in secondary and tertiary parts in films like WOLFEN (1981) and BLADE RUNNER (1982). In the

Eddie Velez in ROMERO

Edward James Olmos in MIAMI VICE

former, he declined to depict a Native American (who turns into a werewolf) until the producers looked for and failed to find an Indian actor, then received the approval of the American Indian Movement.

In 1982, Olmos starred in THE BALLAD OF GREGORIO CORTEZ, a turn-of-the-century tale about a Mexican-American farm worker whose false murder accusation triggers the largest manhunt in Texas history. The picture was shown on PBS and has achieved a cult status. Olmos spent two years marketing and distributing it to theaters around the country because "It could enhance Latino pride all over America." (Olmos' great-uncle had coined the phrase "Tierra y Libertad" [Land and Liberty], which became the rallying cry of the Mexican Revolution.)

Olmos joined the cast of TV's "Miami Vice" as Lt. Martin Castillo in 1984. The role made him a household face and garnered an Emmy and a Golden Globe, plus landed him on the cover of *Time* magazine in a 1988 issue devoted to the "Surging New Spirit of Hispanic Culture." Later in the year, Olmos gained 40 pounds and underwent two hours a day of makeup and "hair-balding" to play real-life math instructor Jaime Escalante in STAND AND DELIVER.

Lou Diamond Phillips and Jaime Escalante

228

Scenes from STAND AND DELIVER, starring Edward James Olmos and Lou Diamond Phillips

The role of an East L.A. high school teacher who motivates his unruly students and improves their grades and lives earned Olmos a 1989 Oscar nomination for Best Actor. He also served as a producer of the unanimously praised movie, directed by Ramon Menendez and co-starring Lou Diamond Phillips, Rosana De Soto and Andy Garcia.

In 1989, Olmos portrayed a gypsy in the grim but uplifting TRIUMPH OF THE SPIRIT, made on location at the former concentration camp of Auschwitz. About his steady employment, he informed *Movieline* magazine, "If Latin American actors are working, it's got an economic basis. We spend more on entertainment per capita five to one than Anglos, and we drink $2^{1}/_{2}$ beers to every one of theirs."

Though Hispanic-themed films of the 1980s tended to improve in quality, they didn't increase in quantity. What set the decade apart, as far as Hispanics were concerned, was the sudden profusion of Hispanic and part-Hispanic performers on the big screen, in both Latin and general roles. A handful of these actors—Andy Garcia, Jimmy Smits, Emilio Estevez and Charlie Sheen—are already stars, and several others look to have a chance at making a lasting impact on Hollywood. Here, a brief "Lat Pack" sampling:

• ANDY GARCIA stood out as Angel Maldonado, a murderous drug kingpin in EIGHT MILLION WAYS TO DIE, and appeared in THE MEAN SEASON, THE UNTOUCHABLES, STAND AND DELIVER, BLACK RAIN (with Michael Douglas), INTERNAL AFFAIRS (as

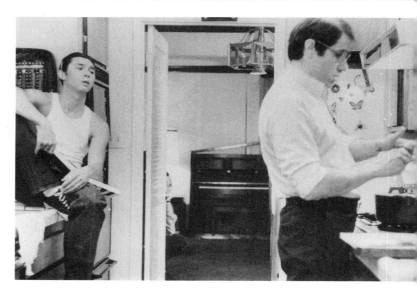

Edward James Olmos in TRI-
UMPH OF THE SPIRIT (1989)

Detective Raymond Avila, opposite Richard Gere; Garcia co-wrote the script) and THE GODFATHER, PART III, as Al Pacino's illegitimate son. For cable TV, he starred as a nickle-and-dime detective in the erotic CLINTON AND NADINE.

"I don't negate that I'm Spanish," says Garcia, born in Cuba, "but I'm not a Spanish actor. No one asks Dustin Hoffman, 'How do you feel representing the Jewish community in Hollywood?'"

• JIMMY SMITS became a household name on "L.A. Law" as Victor Sifuentes, and was seen on the big screen in RUNNING SCARED (with Billy Crystal), John Schlesinger's THE BELIEVERS (with Martin Sheen) and Marisa Silver's VITAL SIGNS (as the dean of third-year studies at a large medical school). He co-starred with Jane Fonda and Gregory Peck in THE OLD GRINGO.

"There are many wonderful Latino stories to be told, but I don't want to get pigeonholed into playing Latinos for the rest of my life."

• EMILIO ESTEVEZ reverted to his father Martin Sheen's original surname and became a mainstream star—with blond hair and blue eyes—in such "Brat Pack" movies (with Rob Lowe, Molly Ringwald, etc.) as THE OUTSIDERS, ST. ELMO'S FIRE, THAT WAS THEN . . . THIS IS NOW, REPO MAN, and WISDOM, which he also directed. With his younger brother Charlie Sheen, he co-starred in YOUNG GUNS and its sequel. With his dad, he starred in TV's NIGHTBREAKER, playing his father as a young man. "I'm interested in the overall picture, and in helping shape it, which is why I got into directing movies and writing them."

• CHARLIE SHEEN has brown eyes and dark hair, and has become a leading screen sex symbol, starting with RED DAWN through the Oscar-winning PLATOON (as new soldier Chris Taylor), WALL

230

Paul Sorvino, Stacy Keach, Robert Mitchum, Bruce Dern and Martin Sheen in THAT CHAMPIONSHIP SEASON (1982)

STREET (with Michael Douglas), NO MAN'S LAND, John Sayles' EIGHT MEN OUT, MAJOR LEAGUE, CADENCE (with Martin Sheen) and MEN AT WORK (with Emilio Estevez).

• ELIZABETH PEÑA played memorable live-in Latina maids in the hit comedy DOWN AND OUT IN BEVERLY HILLS and the TV series "I Married Dora." She appeared in Luis Valdez's LA BAMBA, Peter Bogdanovich's THEY ALL LAUGHED, TIMES SQUARE, FOUND MONEY, BATTERIES NOT INCLUDED and BLUE STEEL. Labeled by one journalist as a "latter-day Lupe Velez," Peña is often squandered in stormy-Latina roles, as in the psychic comedy VIBES, starring Cyndi Lauper and Jeff Goldblum, set in the Ecuadorean Andes.

• LOU DIAMOND PHILLIPS hit it big as early rock star Ritchie Valens in LA BAMBA, then rode the wave with RENEGADES, DISORGANIZED CRIME, YOUNG GUNS, STAND AND DELIVER and A SHOW OF FORCE, the true story of government and police corruption in one of Puerto Rico's biggest scandals; Phillips played undercover agent Jesus Maria "Chucho" Fuentes.

• ROSANA DE SOTO appeared in THE BALLAD OF GREGORIO CORTEZ, then broke through in the crossover hit LA BAMBA, and was seen in STAND AND DELIVER and as Dustin Hoffman's *non*-Hispanic

Hector Elizondo and Martin Sheen in OUT OF THE DARKNESS (1985)

231

Sophia Loren and Hector Elizondo in the telefilm COURAGE (1986)

Telly Savalas and Hector Elizondo in a KOJAK TV movie

wife in FAMILY BUSINESS (wherein Sean Connery played Hoffman's father). "Crosscasting is more common than it used to be," she allows. "Hollywood is realizing that talent isn't limited to a particular nationality, color or heritage."

• RUBEN BLADES, besides being an actor, is a singer-composer (for that matter, Edward James Olmos also began as a musician). His first and most vivid role was in CROSSOVER DREAMS, as a gifted salsa musician who forsakes his Hispanic roots after his first crossover success. Leon Ichaso directed the movie set in Spanish Harlem. Blades was seen in Robert Redford's flop THE MILAGRO BEANFIELD WAR and as Whoopi Goldberg's police partner Carl Jimenez in FATAL BEAUTY.

In Jack Nicholson's THE TWO JAKES, the sequel to CHINATOWN, Blades essayed a 1940s Jewish gangster: "I'm sure somebody must have said, 'Jack, there are a lot of Jews in Hollywood that need a job, why are you going to a Panamanian?'"

• MARIA CONCHITA ALONSO, a Cuban singer-actress, co-starred in the Robin Williams comedy hit MOSCOW ON THE HUDSON, and also EXTREME PREJUDICE, Blake Edwards' A FINE MESS, THE RUN-

Emilio Estevez

NING MAN, THE VAMPIRE'S KISS, TOUCH AND GO and the controversial gang warfare drama set in L.A. and directed by Dennis Hopper, COLORS.

• ESAI MORALES was tagged for stardom as Ritchie Valens' troubled half-brother Bob Morales in LA BAMBA, (he originally had been cast to play Valens). His first role was Sean Penn's Hispanic nemesis in BAD BOYS. The graduate of New York's High School of the Performing Arts (made famous in FAME) appeared on stage in SHORT EYES and in the films FORTY DEUCE, RAINY DAY FRIENDS, BLOODHOUNDS OF BROADWAY (with Madonna) and NAKED TANGO. Also the mini-series ON WINGS OF EAGLES with Burt Lancaster.

Says Morales, "I want to be an actor. Period. They don't call Robert De Niro and Al Pacino famous Italian actors."

• DAPHNE ZUÑIGA shared the small screen with Lucille Ball in the latter's first dramatic telefilm, STONE PILLOW (as a bag lady). She played the spoiled Princess Vespa in Mel Brooks' SPACEBALLS, was the leading lady in THE FLY II, and appeared in Lee Grant's STAYING TOGETHER, Rob Reiner's THE SURE THING (with a memorable beer-chugging

Ally Sheedy, Judd Nelson, Emilio Estevez, Demi Moore, Rob Lowe, Mare Winningham and Andrew McCarthy in ST. ELMO'S FIRE (1985)

scene) and was a first-year med student in GROSS ANATOMY. The half-Guatemalan has been called "regal yet earthy, one of films' most promising newcomers."

• ROBERT BELTRAN starred in Haskell Wexler's LATINO, about the Nicaraguan civil war between the Sandinista regime and Contra rebels. He played an American soldier who is humiliated by being paraded nude before his captors. He was seen, to a lesser extent, in NIGHT OF THE COMET and Paul Bartel's campy comedies EATING RAOUL and SCENES FROM THE CLASS STRUGGLE IN BEVERLY HILLS, in which he enacted a rich woman's servant and would-be seducer named Juan.

• TRINI ALVARADO debuted in pictures at 11 in RICH KIDS and went on to considerable television

Charlie Sheen in PLATOON (1986)

Charlie Sheen in COURAGE MOUNTAIN (1990)

Andy Garcia

work interspersed with films like MRS. SOFFEL (as Diane Keaton's daughter), the musical TIMES SQUARE, SWEET LORRAINE, THE CHAIR, SATISFACTION and STELLA (as Bette Midler's daughter in the STELLA DALLAS remake).

The first half of the 1980s saw few major Hispanic-themed films, although movies set in Latin America were becoming more frequent due to the absorbing political situations in Central and South America. Occasional pictures dealt with Hispanic-Americans or immigrants, but the first of these, THE BORDER (1982, directed by Englishman Tony Richardson), was a Jack Nicholson vehicle criticized as "an exploitive potboiler" by reviewer Gregg Barrios. Nicholson played Charlie Smith, a border patrolman married to blonde, materialistic Valerie Perrine. After he arrests a group of immigrants caught crossing the border, Smith encounters young widow Elpidia Carrillo, whose innocent beauty and simplicity touch him as no one has before.

THE BORDER illuminates injustice within the U.S. Border Patrol, to which Smith has recently transferred, in El Paso, Texas. At first, he is appalled by the cruel hassling of "wetbacks" and the bribes taken by patrolmen who turn their backs while greedy businessmen smuggle in terrified customers who have paid for the border ride with their life-savings.

Andy Garcia and Michael Douglas in BLACK RAIN (1989)

Richard Gere and Andy Garcia in INTERNAL AFFAIRS (1990)

Ana Alicia and company in ROMERO

Robert Beltran

But gradually, Smith begins taking bribes, and comes to despise his greedy, ambitious wife. He is finally propelled to action, and to helping the immigrants, when Carrillo's baby is stolen from her to be sold to a childless, affluent American couple.

The bloody shootout ending, however, recalls a bygone B-Western, and is a less-than-satisfactory climax to a film Stanley Kauffmann of *The New Republic* said "features Jack Nicholson's best performance since ONE FLEW OVER THE CUCKOO'S NEST." Others said it was the closest Nicholson came to playing a man of the people, or that the movie "successfully invades Peckinpah country" or was "a brilliant message picture." Said Nicholson, "You can't change the world, but movies can make us think."

236

Ray Sharkey and Robert Beltran in SCENES FROM THE CLASS STRUGGLE IN BEVERLY HILLS (1989)

Bette Midler and Trini Alvarado in STELLA (1990)

Steven Bauer in GLEAMING THE CUBE (1989)

Costa-Gavras' MISSING (1982) won international kudos for its reality-based plot, its pacing and the performances of Jack Lemmon and Sissy Spacek as Americans searching for his son and her husband—a victim of the partly U.S.-engineered overthrow of Chilean president Allende. Of necessity made in Mexico, MISSING harrowingly spotlights the personal torment and abuses caused by political instability and oppression in any number of Latin nations. The following year, UNDER FIRE cast Nick Nolte and Joanna Cassidy as journalists embroiled in the 1979 Sandinista revolution in Nicaragua (it too was shot in Mexico).

El Salvador during the tumultuous years of 1980-81 was captured in SALVADOR (1986), co-written and directed by Oliver Stone. The events are seen through the eyes and lens of an American photojournalist, searingly portrayed by James Woods. The already-cited LATINO (1985) covered the aftermath of the anti-Somoza uprising through the eyes of an American soldier (Robert Beltran). Writer-director Gregory Nava chose an apolitical point of view for his EL NORTE (1984), about a brother and sister departing troubled Guatemala for the U.S.

He also declined to seek stars like Robby Benson or Brooke Shields for commercial purposes, or to make the characters lovers rather than siblings.

Daphne Zuñiga and John Cusack in THE SURE THING (1985)

Lou Diamond Phillips in LA BAMBA (1987)

And he filmed EL NORTE (The North) in Spanish and was able to bask in the glowing praise for the small-scale hit.

SCARFACE was a 1983 remake by Brian De Palma which strayed far from its source, highlighting the connection between certain Cuban immigrants to Florida and the high-stakes cocaine industry. Al Pacino was the physically and morally damaged anti-hero, cleverly named Tony Montana—"not *too* Hispanic," said one of the film's producers. (SCARFACE had more than one Italian-American playing Hispanic, among them Mary Elizabeth Mastrantonio and Robert Loggia). Within weeks of landing, Montana rises financially from fast-food laborer to crime boss, juggling hit-jobs, two mistresses (one of them his sister, Mastrantonio) and his best friend and right-hand man (half-Cuban Steven Bauer), whom he eventually kills (the two leads were

Lou Diamond Phillips, Esai Morales and player in LA BAMBA

Rosana De Soto and Esai Morales in LA BAMBA

Esai Morales

embodied in the 1932 original—not as Hispanics, of course—by Paul Muni and George Raft).

Due to its popularity, SCARFACE briefly revived the gangster genre, and drew aficionados of almost-X-rated violence. *Vanity Fair* magazine noted, "According to (scenarist) Oliver Stone, Salvadoran death-squad partisans love Pacino's Commie-killing coke king." And, "One recently convicted Long Island drug kingpin loved Tony Montana too much for his own good. He actually used the name, and somewhat foolishly laundered his profits through enterprises called Montana Cleaners and the Montana Sporting Goods Store." Ironic that a film allegedly glorifying the results of crime indirectly helped to apprehend a criminal!

Though helmed by John Huston and starring Britishers Albert Finney, Jacqueline Bisset and Anthony Andrews, UNDER THE VOLCANO (1984) had much more Hispanic input than SCARFACE. Its screenplay, from Malcolm Lowry's celebrated 1947 novel, was by Guy Gallo, its cinematography (called "Goya-like") by Gabriel Figueroa, and it featured Katy Jurado as the owner of a bar-brothel, Rene Ruiz as a malicious dwarf, and Emilio Fernandez as a seedy character named Diosdado (God-given).

The picture spans the last day of life—on the Mexican Day of of the Dead—of Firmin, the British ex-consul in Cuernavaca, and follows his alcoholic ramblings through a picturesque if macabre

and, in the end violent and gruesome, Mexican landscape. Firmin/Finney is killed in the Dante-esque El Farolito bar-brothel by a gang of cut-throats who reflect the era when the novel was written. Curious, that the Mexican government co-financed the film, whose criminals could have been lifted from Huston's THE TREASURE OF THE SIERRA MADRE. *California* magazine pointed out, "Ruiz's portrait of the satanic dwarf who runs the cantina is the most unforgettable Mexican baddie since Gold Hat and his gang" in SIERRA MADRE.

Unlike the book, the film didn't achieve anywhere near cult, let alone profitable, status.

A less grim, though circumscribed, slice of Mexican life was displayed in DOÑA HERLINDA AND HER SON (1986), Mexico's first gay-themed feature. Written and directed by Jaime Humberto Hermosillo, it was in Spanish, but with subtitles became a small-scale hit in the U.S., where its momism and gentle humor struck a responsive chord. *New*

Lou Diamond Phillips

239

Lou Diamond Phillips in RENEGADES (1989)

York's David Denby designated it "A sly, deadpan comedy—the ultimate gay homage to Mom."

Marco Antonio Treviño and Arturo Meza are the two lovers who rearrange their schedules and living arrangements around the former's mother (Guadalupe Del Toro). When Mamacita decides her son should get married, he does, but keeps his lifemate. And still keeps him, in spite of the lover's restiveness, after becoming a father so as to carry on Mamacita's family's name . . . DOÑA HERLINDA was advertised so: "From the Land of the Margarita, the Nacho, the Taco and the Macho" and "A Delicious New Tropical Comedy Treat." The film's logo was an egg containing the male pair, directly beneath a mother hen wearing a sombrero, as she clucks, "Olé!" (On videocassette, DOÑA HERLINDA is reportedly the best-selling-ever Mexican movie in the American market.)

EL NORTE and DOÑA HERLINDA were among the precious few films from south of the border to spark gold at the U.S. box office. Specialized pictures for urban movie buffs, they had far less to lose than a studio movie which tried to appeal to everyone and wound up pleasing no one. Such was the case with THE MILAGRO BEANFIELD WAR (1987), about a lone Chicano (Chick Vennera) who opposes a development project in his virtual backyard. But

Lou Diamond Phillips and Kiefer Sutherland in RENEGADES

ere long, his enthusiasm infects the entire village, and they join his environmental crusade, which also has cultural undertones. As literature, it worked beautifully. But neither Robert Redford nor probably anyone else could have converted the material into a cohesive cinematic whole.

MILAGRO comes off dull and predictable, and didn't draw flies at the box office, losing multi-millions and reinforcing Hollywood thinking that Latino laborers and profits don't mix. Long before it was released, a storm of controversy had arisen over the fact that a non-Hispanic was directing the screen version (which likely wouldn't have gotten funding without Redford) and casting non-Hispanic actors in many of the speaking parts.

But that same year, came LA BAMBA, shattering the myths, and launching or firming several careers. For starters, there was the title song, which has been called the Chicano national anthem. Composed in Veracruz, Mexico, in the early 19th century, "La Bamba" was recorded in 1959 by a talented Pacoima, California, teenager named Ritchie Valens (né Richie Valenzuela), whose bittersweet story this is. (On the flip side of the rock 'n roller's record was his own doo-wop composition, "Donna," which was an even bigger hit.)

Written and directed by ZOOT SUIT's Luis Valdez, the movie had something for everyone—attractive and talented young performers, sexual and musical energy, the drama of familial and love relationships, the "color" of minority culture, and tragedy, for Valens died at 17 in an airplane crash with fellow rocker Buddy Holly (who'd already been successfully biographed in THE BUDDY HOLLY STORY). Australia's *Screensight* magazine stated, "Music truly is the universal language, and nothing succeeds like excess in a singing career. The singer who

Rita Hayworth, Cesar Romero and Dolores Del Rio: the last party ever attended by Hayworth and Del Rio, in 1982

Dolores Del Rio's last public appearance, in 1982

Univision TV host Luca Bentivoglio with Mexican actor Jorje Rivero

Rene Enriquez of HILL STREET BLUES

finishes tragically is a film staple going back several decades.

"This is the first such bio of a Hispanic singer . . . Via its toe-tapping, highly danceable rhythms, LA BAMBA engages audience sympathy for Valens as an individual and for his family and compatriots as a group."

LA BAMBA was a shot in the arm for Hispanic Hollywood on both sides of the camera. Latin directors were finally being let in, e.g., EL NORTE's Gregory Nava went on to A TIME OF DESTINY; PIXOTE's Hector Babenco helmed Nicholson and Meryl Streep in IRONWEED; Jane Fonda imported Luis Puenzo, director of the Oscar-winning THE OFFICIAL STORY, from Argentina for THE OLD GRINGO. And it took LA BAMBA, though a lesser hit than the 1977 SATURDAY NIGHT FEVER, to inspire SALSA (1988), which

numerous critics termed "the Hispanic SATURDAY NIGHT FEVER."

Robby Rosa is SALSA's Travolta, a handsome, self-centered Puerto Rican grease monkey who dreams of becoming the "King of Salsa" in a dance contest at a Los Angeles nightclub. His obsession with dancing brings him into conflict with his girlfriend, his family and his pal (Rodney Harvey). But it pays off in—did you ever doubt it?—the royal title and a frenzy of orgiastic crotch-dancing which brought in the teenage audience (in one scene, Angela Alvarado leads Rosa around the dance floor by his genitals). SALSA, like another dance hit, DIRTY DANCING, offers no issues or cultural insights, only vertical sexuality. If anything, the movie's real star is Kenny Ortega's choreography.

Finally, 1989 saw the release of the $24-million

Gregory Peck was the old Gringo, journalist Ambrose Bierce—who disappeared at age 71 while covering the Revolution in 1914. (Burt Lancaster was to have played Bierce, before health problems intervened.)

Jimmy Smits portrayed Tomas Arroyo, a general in Villa's army. The character serves a dual purpose in the movie. He unleashes the repressed passions of the virginal Winslow, and represents a divided Mexico, torn asunder by un-civil strife. Although he supports the goals of the Revolution, Arroyo, "a composite of different figures, is paralyzed by his past," said Smits. The son of a wealthy landowner, he is both repelled and fascinated by his aristocratic position. His materialism proves too strong for him

Stereotypes in CROCODILE DUNDEE II (1988): left, the hero confronts Garcia (Carlos Carrasco); right, the heroine is confronted by Miguel (Juan Fernandez)

epic THE OLD GRINGO, from the novel *El Gringo Viejo* by Carlos Fuentes. Producer Jane Fonda explained, "When I met Carlos in 1980, I told him my dream was to make a movie about the relationship between my country and his, one that doesn't smooth over the differences but unshrinkingly confronts them."

Fonda enacted one of three strangers who get to know each other well and learn more about themselves in 1913 Mexico while anticipating Pancho Villa and watching the Revolution rage about them. Fonda played schoolteacher Harriet Winslow, and

Gregory Peck, Jane Fonda and Jimmy Smits in THE OLD GRINGO (1989)

Jimmy Smits and Gregory Peck in THE OLD GRINGO

to continue with Villa's army after he has captured a comfortable hacienda, where he sequesters himself.

Shot entirely on location in Mexico, the movie has considerable Spanish-language dialogue. "This was done to make it more naturalistic," declared Fonda, "to mirror the perplexity and barriers each culture feels when confronted with alien people and their tongue." But despite the effort put into the often breathtakingly beautiful film, it was not a hit. Perhaps, again, it wasn't specific enough. Fonda noted, "You can take OLD GRINGO as an adventure, as a profound political statement, or a love story of sorts." Alas, Pancho Villa and the Revolution—and even its American adherents—had finally lost their box office luster.

"The combined star power of Fonda, Peck and Smits cannot counter America's indifference to his-torically-minded films," said *Premiere* magazine, which might have added that domestic audiences shun even the rare pictures about U.S. history, such as the 1986 REVOLUTION (American, that is), star-ring Al Pacino and made in Britain. Jane Fonda later stated, "OLD GRINGO was made as much for the Hispanic market outside of the United States as it was for American audiences.

"After decades of Hollywood treating Latin America with contempt on the screen, I'm glad that our movie at least made an attempt to treat our neighbors to the south as equals and friends."

As this book goes to press, a movie casting deci-sion has just been made which most of Hollywood is buzzing about. Robert Redford is making one of his periodic acting comebacks, in HAVANA. Never mind that the combination of name-star and exotic setting fizzles at the box office more often than not. For months, Hollywood has been speculating who would get to pick off the plum role of the fiery Cubana opposite Redford. Were the film to suc-ceed, the role could conceivably create a star. Or make a star into a bigger star.

Who would it be? Maria Conchita Alonso? Or Elizabeth Peña? How about Sonia Braga? Or Rosana De Soto?

The role has gone to Lena Olin—a Swede.

Britisher David Puttnam, the ex-Columbia stu-

THE OLD GRINGO: Gregory Peck, Jimmy Smits, star-producer Jane Fonda, director Luis Puenzo and author Carlos Fuentes

Tab Hunter and Cesar Romero in LUST IN THE DUST (1985)

Why, it has been well asked, is a film like THE OLD GRINGO, about the Mexican Revolution, considered "ethnic," even when its two top stars aren't? And why are films about the French Revolution not considered ethnic?

What's changed in America? A lot. There are now Hispanic mayors, senators and governors. On dio boss who once criticized Hollywood for not embracing its ethnic richness has, as a producer, recently chosen Glenn Close and William Hurt for the leads in his HOUSE OF THE SPIRITS, from Isabel Allende's novel set in Argentina, nearly as alien as starring Roy Scheider and Liv Ullmann in TV's JACOBO TIMMERMAN: PRISONER WITHOUT A NAME, CELL WITHOUT A NUMBER (about the activist Argentine newspaper publisher).

Warner Bros. is preparing an eagerly awaited adventure/bio film about Francisco Chico Mendes, the South American rain forest preservationist murdered for taking up that cause which has become ecology-minded Hollywood's favorite. The bidding war for screen rights to the Mendes project was fierce and costly; the movie budget will begin at $22 million. Who will play Mendes? At the moment, the leading contenders are Dustin Hoffman, Robert De Niro and Al Pacino.

What's changed in Hollywood? A lot. Ricardo Mestres, a Hispanic, heads Disney's Hollywood Pictures, the first such studio executive with the power to "green-light" a motion picture. But will he initiate or give the go-ahead to any Hispanic-themed films? Or cast Hispanic actors in major Hispanic roles?

Gilbert Roland in BARBAROSA (1982)

Steven Bauer in SWORD OF GIDEON (1986)

the other hand, says Mexican-American comic Paul Rodriguez, "I could talk about a John DeLorean, who got busted with a suitcase of cocaine on video-tape and he got out, and I have three friends who are doing better than 30 years for stealing a car . . ."

Over a third of Los Angeles' population is Hispanic. Its more than three million Latinos make it the second-largest Spanish-speaking city in the world, after Mexico City, the largest city in any language. It's estimated that a decade from now, Los Angeles, including geographic Hollywood, will be over half-Hispanic. But there's Hollywood, and there's Hollywood:

In 1969, Ricardo Montalban led a group of actors who founded NOSOTROS, initially dedicated to protesting the sorts of roles Hispanic actors had to take, and more recently devoted to bettering the image of Hispanics in Hollywood films. The same year, 1969, a U.S. Equal Employment Opportunity Commission report found that only three percent of Hollywood studios' employees had Spanish surnames. Incredibly, public television's record was worse—under one percent! This, in the City of

Elizabeth Peña and Jeff Goldblum in VIBES (1988)

247

Angels, the mecca of Mexican immigrants and growing numbers of Central Americans, Colombians and others.

Have these figures since improved? Apparently, not much. Equal Opportunity reports and programs under the current and last presidential administrations have been few, and show that the new Hollywood isn't that different from the old. Not behind the screen or off the sound-stages, at any rate.

How many people, even in Hollywood, know that there are over 450 Spanish-language movie theaters in the United States? Or that the U.S. Hispanic market accounts for 40 percent of the exports

Magali Alvarado and Rodney Harvey in SALSA (1988)

of Mexico's film industry, Latin America's largest, which for decades has successfully sold celluloid product to Spain, Argentina and more than a dozen other nations?

Obviously, there is strength in numbers, and when those numbers are growing this fast—for, Hispanics are already America's biggest minority, apart from men—it's only a matter of time. But numbers alone are passive; influence, creativity and deliberate, thoughtful change are active results of

249

Edward James Olmos in THE BALLAD OF GREGORIO CORTEZ (1982)

duction's opening quote, sheer numbers mean Hollywood will have to pay more attention to the Hispanic market. Who, however, will shape and create the products which go to that and to all markets? Why do Hispanic stars of breakthrough hits like LA BAMBA and STAND AND DELIVER usually fail to find followup hits? And why do so many Hispanic actors of all ages still demur, when offered a recognizably ethnic part? Clearly, much has changed, but much has not.

Edward James Olmos, Rose Portillo and Daniel Valdez in ZOOT SUI (1981)

individual power and will. Why have so many of the misrepresentative and even the good Hispanic-themed films over the decades been written and directed by non-Latinos? Why, when there's a current explosion of Hispanic performers of every description, are there still so few Hispanic filmmakers?

As Edward James Olmos stated earlier in this chapter, the power of Hispanics' entertainment dollars is good for the Hispanic actor looking for work. And as Ricardo Montalban said in the intro-

Al Pacino in SCARFACE (1983)

Albert Finney, Jacqueline Bisset and Anthony Andrews in UNDER THE VOLCANO

Hopefully, this book has given an indication of the general range and personal fluctuations of Hollywood's Hispanic stars. And of the depth and frequent lack thereof of Hollywood's depictions of Hispanic characters.

Hispanic Hollywood has come far indeed. With far yet to go. It has had more than its share of glamour, disappointment, excitement, injustice, controversy and hopeful change. More than its share, in fact, of most everything under the glaring, seductive and worldwide Hollywood sun.

Everything, except perhaps self-determination and -definition. So far . . .

Albert Finney and Katy Jurado in UNDER THE VOLCANO

Bibliography

Anger, Kenneth. "Hollywood Babylon." New York: Bell Publishing Co., 1981.

Arnaz, Desi. "A Book." New York: William Morrow and Co., 1976.

Baxter, John. "Hollywood in the Thirties." New York: A.S. Barnes and Co., 1968.

Biberman, Herbert. "Salt of the Earth." Boston: Beacon Press, 1965.

Brown, Peter H., and Jim Pinkston. "Oscar Dearest." New York: Harper and Row, 1987.

Christensen, Terry. "Reel Politics." New York: Basil Blackwell, 1987.

Everson, William K. "The Bad Guys." New York: Citadel Press, 1964.

Horwitz, James. "They Went Thataway—Old-Time Hollywood Cowboys." New York: E.P. Dutton, 1976.

Hyams, Jay. "The Life and Times of the Western Movie." New York: Gallery Books, 1983.

Keller, Gary D., ed. "Chicano Cinema." Binghamton, New York: Bilingual Review Press, 1985.

Keyser, Les. "Hollywood in the Seventies." La Jolla, California: A.S. Barnes, 1981.

Marill, Alvin H. "The Films of Anthony Quinn." Secaucus, New Jersey: Citadel Press, 1975.

McClelland, Doug. "Hollywood on Hollywood." Boston: Faber and Faber, 1985.

Miller, Randall M., ed. "The Kaleidoscopic Lens—How Hollywood Views Ethnic Groups." Englewood, New Jersey: Jerome S. Ozer, Publisher, 1980.

Mora, Carl J. "Mexican Cinema." Berkeley: University of California Press, 1982.

Null, Gary. "Black Hollywood." Secaucus, New Jersey: Citadel Press, 1975.

Pettit, Arthur G. "Images of the Mexican-American in Fiction and Film." College Station, Texas: A&M University Press, 1980.

Quart, Leonard, and Albert Auster. "American Film and Society Since 1945." New York: Praeger, 1984.

Quinn, Anthony. "The Original Sin." Boston: Little, Brown, 1972.

Ringgold, Gene. "The Films of Rita Hayworth." Secaucus, New Jersey: Citadel Press, 1974.

Roffman, Peter, and Jim Purdy. "The Hollywood Social Problem Film." Bloomington, Indiana: Indiana University Press, 1981.

Rothel, David. "Those Great Cowboy Sidekicks." Metuchen, New Jersey: Scarecrow Press, 1984.

St. Charnez, Casey. "The Films of Steve McQueen." Secaucus, New Jersey: Citadel Press, 1984.

Westmore, Frank, and Muriel Davidson. "The Westmores of Hollywood." Philadelphia: Lippincott, 1976.

Woll, Allen L. "The Latin Image in American Film." Los Angeles: UCLA Latin American Series, 1977.

INDEX

254